"At this time when there is so much violence, conflict, terrorism, and division, beginning from the family to the international community, this book comes as a timely masterpiece to address these issues. The author's masterly use of the Scriptures to critique and correct the current status quo makes it convincing that peaceful coexistence is possible in Nigeria and elsewhere. The depth of scholarship and simplicity of language commend this volume as a must read."

—**Donatus Udoette**, Uyo Catholic Diocese, Nigeria

"Multifaceted problems in religion and society are caused by humans who have lost touch with what it means to be human. If these problems are to be resolved, these responsible agents need to be repositioned to reclaim their true identity as people created in God's 'image and likeness.' . . . Fr. Udoekpo is to be very highly commended for painstakingly illustrating this truth and offering sustainable solutions."

—**Teresa Okure**, SHCJ, Catholic Institute of West Africa, Nigeria

"Fr. Mike Ufok has successfully woven together those social factors which inhibit the search for ethics and unity in Nigeria and globally, factors such as corruption, injustice, oppression, kidnappings, terrorism, crimes, fear, unemployment, human degradation, and the rising tide of atheistic secularism. . . . He is able to proffer a remedial process of returning to core family values and the rule of law. . . . Highly recommended for both academics and policy makers."

—**Basil A. Ekot**, Veritas University Abuja, Nigeria

"Insightful and analytical in nature. Dr. Michael Udoekpo gives the reader deep and clear root causes of human failures as an individual and as a society and proposes a spiritual and moral revolution that ought to start immediately from within."

—**Anselm Camillus Etokakpan**, University of Uyo, Nigeria

"This multifaceted study wades into the causes of conflict and disharmony in the world, and particularly Nigeria, and emerges unscarred with concrete proposals on how to deal with them. The author exemplifies this with select texts from the Bible and in-depth analysis of the role of the family, mass media, and politics in guaranteeing the stability of any nation. In a society marked by incessant conflicts and threats of war, I highly recommend this book."

—**Emmanuel O. Nwaoru**, Catholic Institute of West Africa, Nigeria

The Limits of a Divided Nation with Perspectives from the Bible

To: Very Rev. Fr. Raúl Gómez- Ruiz

From: Fr. Michael Ufok Udoekpo

with Gratitude

2/25/2020

The Limits of a Divided Nation with Perspectives from the Bible

MICHAEL UFOK UDOEKPO

Forewords by DONATUS UDOETTE
and CAROLINE N. MBONU, HHCJ
Epilogue by ANSELM CAMILLUS ETOKAKPAN

RESOURCE *Publications* · Eugene, Oregon

To all who hunger and thirst for peaceful coexistence in the world and to those who for 25 years have encouraged me in my priestly ministry

Contents

Foreword I by Donatus Udoette | ix

Foreword II by Caroline N. Mbonu, HHCJ | xv

Acknowledgements | xix

Introduction | 1

1 Social Power of the Family and Unity | 7

2 Wars in Religious Families and Their Limits | 24

3 The Mismanagement of Politics and Unity | 39

4 Effects of the Abuse of Mass Media on the Quest for Unity | 44

5 Lessons from Micah's Corruption in Judges 17:1–6 | 54

6 Unity from the Perspectives of Luke 3:4–6 and Isaiah 40:4–5 | 70

7 Unity from the Perspectives of Romans 14:1–15:13 | 85

   A Modest Conclusion | 93

Epilogue by Anselm Camillus Etokakpan | 97

Bibliography | 101

Index of Authors | 109

Index of Scriptures | 111

Index of Subjects | 117

Foreword I

I AM HAPPY TO be asked again by Rev. Fr. Michael Ufok Udoekpo to write another foreword for the second and expanded edition of his book on *The Limits of a Divided Nation*. As I look back to 1999 when the book was first published, I acknowledge with deep admiration and satisfaction the new insights which the author has brought into the new edition, thanks to his growth in scholarship as well as the experience, both pastoral and otherwise, which have helped to shape his thinking and focus. There is no doubt that many things have changed in Nigeria and in the entire world since 1999, and therefore the limits of a nation that is so divided is obviously not the same again. If the author had wanted, he would have completely dropped the first edition of his book and write a new one, following the changes and happenings that have taken place after the first edition was published. He has however, chosen to expand and enrich what he published in 1999.

In Nigeria in particular new realities, both good and bad, have probed up on the terrain of our divided nation. On the positive side, it can be said that the military rule of yesteryears has given space to a nascent democracy that is hopefully crystalizing towards stabilization. Communication network has improved over the years, thanks to the advancements in cyber technology, notwithstanding its ugly side. New infrastructures have been put in place and there is some kind of "new mentality" that is being injected into the polity. The government is fighting and is being fought by corruption. Above all, the happenings of the past years have toughened Nigerians into "thick skinners", thus making them able to weather the storms in good as well as bad times.

On the negative side, a lot of things have also happened in Nigeria since 1999. For example, at the time when the book was first published there was no kidnapping. There was no Boko Haram insurgency, no armed herdsmen carrying AK47 assault rifles, walking about freely, killing, maiming and destroying lives and properties. There was no armed banditry on the highways, making Nigerian roads unsafe for wayfarers. There was not much fear of strangers or strange faces in Nigerian societies, because such persons were regarded as visitors to be welcomed and treated well in accordance with the innate African hospitality. People used to go to bed and sleep with their two eyes closed with little or no fear of possible attacks in the night. But today, all that has changed!

Even though Nigeria as a nation was grossly divided on many fronts—religiously, politically, culturally and ethnically, the ugly realities of the time put together did not build up to the national insomnia and restlessness associated with the level of insecurity that we have today. The magnitude of violence and bloodletting experienced in the country today is unparalleled. Nigeria has become schizophrenic, and anything can happen anytime, any day, any place. Darwinian principle of survival of the fittest has become the rule of life for the poor "jungle dwellers". One can survive only to the extent that he/she is smart enough to outsmart others in the rat race of life that has become ugly, brutish and short.

Furthermore, the political terrain has drastically altered. Some Nigerian politicians today are not helping matters. Rather than assist in the growth and stabilization of the nascent democracy, they have become unrepentant protagonists of stomach-cracy, a government of their stomach, by their stomach and for their stomach. Besides, the rule of engagement in politics for some politicians is simply Machiavellian. Some politicians behave like volcanic eruptions that do not spare anything, alive or dead, on their way. They have their "private armies" in the form of political thugs, whom they recruit from frustrated and unemployed youths in the villages, urban centres and institutions to advance their selfish political agenda. Politics is no longer seen as a means of service, but rather as a visa for power, control, surplus cash and waste. Many politicians of yesteryears have either passed on or have retired from active politics. New political parties and ideologies have been launched; and the socio-economic and cultural terrain have also changed drastically.

Economically, some positive measures have been taken by government to improve the lots of the people. However, the fact still remains that there is a lot of hunger in the land. Many Nigerians today are not sure of one good meal in a day. Currently, the government has tried to close borders in order to check unnecessary importation of what could be produced locally and to encourage and assist local industries. But we still have economic saboteurs who smuggle in expired food items for the consumption of vulnerable Nigerians. They keep importing very low quality and dangerous products into the country. It is a sad and pitiable situation!

One would have expected that education would help to build a new mentality and instil morality and discipline, but this is largely not the case! Private institutions have taken over education from the government. Worse still the children of the rich and influential Nigerians are not studying under the wretched conditions experienced by the children of other Nigerians who cannot afford to send their children across the seas for better education. The result is that public institutions of education are not properly funded and cared for. Teachers are underpaid; many students are only interested in high scores and not in knowledge. On account of greed and for other selfish reasons some teachers exploit and extort from the students. Some students exchange money or sex or both for high scores. At the end of the day the purpose of education which is to train, form and groom responsible citizens becomes frustrated. There are many other things could be said about Nigeria, which was cobbled together many years back by Lord Lugard and his colonial allies. The result of that political arrangement is still telling on Nigeria today.

The new publication titled *The Limits of a Divided Nation with Perspectives from the Bible*, is to a certain extent, self-explanatory. In this edition the author has gone beyond a phenomenological analysis of the problems associated with a beaten and battered nation to making use of the scriptures to interpret and proffer a way out of the ugly quack mire. The problems discussed and discountenanced are not limited to Nigeria alone, but also extend to global issues such as the holocaust and the World Wars, which effects are felt till today. Although the author does not use one single pericope or document from either the Old or the New Testament to critique the current *status quo*, yet he is able to adapt from a diversity of biblical traditions those scriptural passages that broadly and theologically allude or speak directly to contemporary situation. He is disappointed that humankind has up till now not seen the need for peace, unity and mutual coexistence, but has rather given too much space to wars, materialism, terrorism and total breakdown of the tendons that used to hold the society together.

The Limits of a Divided Nation with Biblical Perspectives is made up of seven chapters. In chapter one, the author takes time to analyse the causes of division and disunity from the social perspective. It is his conviction that the social fabric of the society has been battered and distorted. He blames the family as the nucleus of the society for losing its grip on the training, formation and instilling discipline and sound moral values in children. Since many young couples are themselves not formed, and therefore not mature and responsible, the result is that it is impossible to expect that they will exercise the office of responsible parents. Very often parents, consciously or unconsciously, contract out their parental duties to house helps, peer groups and public schools who have nothing good to offer to the children. The family therefore has failed in its duty and has thus contributed to the disunity and the ills that we experience today.

Chapter two of the work deals with the religious divide that is experienced today in Nigeria. There is no peaceful coexistence of Christianity, Islam and African Traditional Religion, which are the three major religions of the country. Religion is supposed to be an instrument of peace and mutual coexistence, but unfortunately it has often been used as a means of division and war. Many Nigerians, both in the past and in the present, have lost their means of livelihood or their lives or both in religious crisis. Much as it is true that some conscienceless politicians sometimes make use of religion as a cover-up for the advancement of their political agenda, yet there are cases in Nigeria where religion sometimes constitutes a powerful dividing force and the cause of violence and bloodletting. The recent activities of the Islamic Movement of Nigeria and its subsequent proscription by government is a case in point.

The role of politics and political power takes the centre stage of the author's adumbration in chapter three. As long as unscrupulous and conscienceless individuals continue to hijack and suffocate the role and purpose of politics as a vehicle of service, peace, security and development, there will be no end to violence and disunity in Nigeria. Is it not possible to bring morality into politics? This is the author's question and challenge to politicians.

In chapter four, the author dwells on the role of mass media in building or destroying any country or polity. Journalists and men and women of the media have a sacred role to play in either fostering peace and unity or destroying same in any given situation. The media is supposed to act as the conscience of the nation, but sometimes by compromising with cantankerous elements and their selfish agenda, it destroys the very polity it is supposed to build. Journalists are to note that the pen in their hand is like a double-edged sword that can cut in two directions. The author thus extends a clarion call to all stake holders in the media to know that they are indebted to the citizenry, and should therefore exhibit a high sense of responsibility in carrying out their duties.

In chapters five, six and seven, the author dwells on what he calls biblical theology of unity. As a scripture scholar he is able to use scriptural passages and pericopes from both the Old and New Testaments to critique the current situation of disunity in Nigeria as well as attempt to proffer solutions. Each chapter ends with a brief summary and conclusion.

In his general conclusion to the issues discussed, the author calls for prayer, proper education, telling and living the truth, restoration of family values, interreligious and cultural dialogue, ecumenism, enforcement of the rule of law, faith in God, etc as a way out of violence, friction and disunity, not only in Nigeria, but also in the entire world.

I congratulate Fr. Michael for finding time, in spite of his crowded schedule, to publish this important work and make it available to the reading public. The beauty of his book is not just in the fact of incorporating new scriptural materials into the previous edition, but in his capacity to handle those materials in a way that ultimately crystalize into a must read. The book is truly a must read, not only for Nigerians, but also for every other person from other climes, precisely because the problems of Nigeria are also largely the problems of the world today. Disunity, violence, terrorism and anarchy are not only experienced in Nigeria; they have become the order of the day in almost all parts of the world. There is racism, violence, division, ethnocentricism, economic and political mess, religious clashes, etc in Nigeria as also in many parts of Africa and the rest of the world today.

This work therefore has implications that go beyond the borders of any given country. It draws attention to the fact that if humankind were ready to embrace and work for peace and mutual coexistence, the World Wars would not have been necessary. The Golf War would have been avoided. The current violence in the Democratic Republic of Congo, the Liberian war, the Sudanese wars, the ethnic clashes in the Cameroons as well as the xenophobic attacks in South Africa and other parts of the world would not have been called for. Racism, division, hatred and ethnocentricism as manifested in some parts of the world today would have been avoided if humankind were ready to embrace the language of peace. The current spate of global terrorism and violence that is unleashing fear and insecurity on the world would not have taken place if humankind were disposed to dialogue and diplomatic resolution of conflicts. These are the issues that make *The Limits of a Divided Nation with Perspectives from the Bible* a must read. I therefore call, not only on scholars from every discipline, but also general readers and lovers of peace to create a space for this book in their shelves.

Very Rev. Fr. Dr. Donatus Udoette
Vicar General, Catholic Diocese of Uyo
Nigeria

Foreword II

THE REQUEST TO WRITE a Foreword to this prodigious piece of work, was a bit of a surprise but a welcome one. Having known and worked closely with the author, Fr. Michael Ufok Udoekpo for over three decades, from his student days as a Claretian at the House of Philosophy, at Maryland Nekede, Owerri, the Catholic diocese of Ikot Ekpene, and our common membership of the several biblical associations. He shows mastery of his subject in the generous weaving of various disciplines, Scripture, politics, theology, social sciences and culture, to produce a tapestry representative of unity and peace in a pluralistic society such as Nigeria and elsewhere. The author makes a case for the family in the African traditional sense of the word. His idea of a family unit as "the first and fundamental school of social living," is at the heart of this profound thesis on unity and peace in any nation. Not only from his life's situation, the author supports his assertion with insights rooted deeply in the Bible, that foundational text of Christianity, which has informed humankind of the worth of individuals and the call to work for peace intentionally as well as fight against evil.

A biblical scholar and a Catholic priest, one engaged fully in teaching biblical studies as well as pastoral ministry, the author stands in a unique position to write this book, *The Limits of a Divided Nation with Perspectives from the Bible that* seeks ways to engender unity and peace among peoples. He grounds his discussion on family: that primal institution in the social order, a "sanctuary of life," and employs family sensitive as thread that runs through the seven chapters, illuminating the discussion.

Since the family remains the building block or root metaphor of a nation, the author left no stone unturned in stressing the unique position of parents in the upbringing of a child; for him, the consequences of a faulty child-rearing portend disaster for a nation and the global community as well. What the author identifies as perennial problems in contemporary Nigeria: bad governance, ethnocentrism in politics, corruption, moral decadence, and other social malaise that fuel disunity cannot be unconnected with untoward experiences in familial structure.

Disunity in Nigeria is not limited to the civil society; religious groups have their share of the canker worm that continues to devastate the land and its people. Christians as well as Moslems are not immune to denominational conflicts. Among Christians, the different Pentecostal-Charismatic groups found in almost every nook and cranny of the country, although appear "to offer security" for followers "in a hostile world," still leaves much to be desired regarding unity with non-members, particularly those of Mainline Christian churches. Moslems fair no better; the Shiite-Sunni conundrum is also taking its toll on unity and peace in the country. The author traces some crises triggered by religious intolerance and calls the Mass Media to account.

Although disunity among religious groups metathesize in the public space, the Mass Media prudent deployment of social community, can assuage instead of fueling an already degenerating situation, the author insists. As image makers, the Mass Media can foster congeniality among the various peoples and persuasively advocate for the common good.

Conversion to a way of life support that common good is *sine qua non* to national unity, a life free of corruption in its various manifestations. The biblical example of Micah and his unnamed mother (Judges 17:1-6) is telling. In addition, the fine exegetical work on the Prophet Isaiah in Babylon and the Gospel according to Luke, hacks back to family, in its extended form of which the metaphor of Church-family is emblematic in the pursuit of national unity. Michael's rendering of Pauline teaching on Unity in Romans (14—15), bares the Christian duty in bringing forth and maintain unity in the community for "The freedom that members of the Church in Africa enjoy is a freedom to tolerate one another;" tolerance that provides an environment where "the weak" and "the strong" can flourish together, a community that continues to reinterpret and live repeatedly the paradox of the weed and the wheat. Living intentionally the paradox of the weeds and the wheats births the peace echoed by the prophet Micah "Every man shall sit under his own vine or under his own fig tree, undisturbed" (4:4), because they shall have learned how to accommodate difference with dignity and respect.

This well researched book on fundamental issues affecting peaceful co-existence in contemporary society, be it in Africa or elsewhere is a must read. With Nigeria as a focus, the challenges that foster unity highlighted in the book militate against development in all its ramifications in any society, Nigeria and elsewhere. This book is an invaluable resource for students in the humanities and social science, and for persons involved in peace-building as well as community development, particularly those who must grapple with a way of being good neighbors in a pluralistic society.

Caroline N. Mbonu, HHCJ, PhD
Department of Religious and Cultural Studies
Faculty of Humanities
University of Port Harcourt, Nigeria
November 2019

Acknowledgements

THIS PUBLICATION COINCIDES WITH my 25th priestly anniversary. I am very grateful to God for the gift of my vocation. I was ordained October 7, 1995 to bring Christ to people and people to Christ. Over the years I have persevered in doing this collaboratively with others in my little way, to the best of my ability, in different parts of the world, Africa, Europe and the United States of America, and in many ways through ministering the sacraments, preaching and writing. This work *The Limits of a Divided Nation with Perspectives from the Bible* is one among the many. For this I am grateful to all those who have supported, prayed for me and encouraged me over the years.

I am particularly grateful to my Bishop Most Rev. Camillus Umoh and Bishop Camillus Etokudoh, our provincial Bishops, brother-priests, religious, family, village community and town's people, friends, parishioners, colleagues and students for all their payers and assistance.

My debts of gratitude also go to all those friends and colleagues who have willingly and cheerfully contributed, endorsed and generously given their time, voice and energy in form of forewords, preface or epilogue to promote and recommend this work to the reading public. I am specifically referring to Very Rev. Dr. Donatus Udoette of the Catholic Diocese of Uyo, Sr. Dr. Caroline N. Mbonu HHCJ, of the University of Port Harcourt, Very Rev. Dr. Anselm Etokakpan of the Catholic Diocese of Ikot Ekpene and Rev. Dr. Basil Ekot of the Veritas Catholic University, Abuja. I am also grateful to Professors Teresa Okure SHCJ and Emmanuel O. Nwaoru of the Catholic Institute of Africa for their highly significant endorsement.

I am also thankful to readers and editors of the manuscript including Ms Elizabeth Vince, Susana Pathak and editorial members of the Resource

Publications. Their editorial insight and comments have tremendously improved the quality of the original draft.

Certainly my debts are numerous; especially to those whose names are not individually mentioned here, yet have played positive roles in my life. I want to say thank you, "May the Lord Bless you and keep you; may the Lord make his face shine upon you, and be gracious to you; may the Lord lift up his countenance upon you and give you peace" (Num 6:24-26).

Fr. Michael Ufok Udoekpo
Associate Professor Biblical Studies
Sacred Heart Seminary and School of Theology
Wisconsin, USA
January 2020

Introduction

It has been nearly two decades since the publication of the first edition of *The Limits of a Divided Nation* (1999) by the Snaap Press, Enugu, Nigeria. At that time, as a newly ordained young Catholic priest without advanced degrees in biblical theology and with limited pastoral experiences, my focus was not only on unity in Nigeria and beyond, but on the causes of disharmony and the way out from such a mess. In this expanded edition, my focus remains fundamentally the same, except it is more biblical and more inclusive both in pastoral language and perspectives. Scriptural insights are intentionally drawn from biblical history, including passages such as Judges 17:1–6; Isaiah 40:4–5; Luke 3:4–6; and Romans 14–15.

In this current edition, in an effort to cherish the past, I have maintained in the most part the language, grammar, content, integrity and the simplicity of the first edition (chaps. 1–4). It was not intended for a rigorous exegetical work for experts alone. In it I pastorally lamented the danger of disunity, conflict, and friction in different fabrics of Nigerian society. This includes families, religious groups, government, and the mass media. I highlighted the causes of such divisions and proposed limited solutions, all within five concise chapters.

Those chapters seemed to have been well received by the public. Currently that edition is out of print. Requests for that edition, especially by my colleagues, students, and the much younger generation, are sources of inspiration for this new project, which also marks the twenty-fifth year of my priestly ordination on October 7, 1995, at St. Ann's Cathedral, Ifuho, Ikot Ekpene Diocese, in Nigeria.

Valuable to that 1999 edition were two forewords. One was from Very Rev. Dr. Donatus Udoette (then Rector of St. Major Seminary, Ikot Ekpene,

1

Nigeria), while the other came from my vocation director, Very Rev. Dr. Silas T. Umoh of the blessed memory (then parish priest at St. Vincent Ikot Obong Edong, Ikot Ekpene, Nigeria).These forewords enhanced my persistent and current reflection that there seems to be a universal belief that there is a limit for everything. It seems that, over the many generations that have passed since Adam and Eve, humanity would have learned the fundamental ethics of peaceful coexistence and the limits of division, corruption, racism, segregation, tribalism, and sociopolitical fragmentation. It seems that humanity would have learned the necessity of searching for unity, justice, and peace that only God can give. They would have put into practice those principles that generate and nurture peace and harmony, simultaneously eliminating all friction and dichotomy. They would have learned to respect the dignity of every human person and of nature.

But from all indications, this is not the case. We are still living in one of the most troubled periods in the history of mankind. Our world is experiencing wars, climate change debates, materialism, secularism, terrorism, increasing divorce rates, and the breakdown of family values. Fundamentalism, sexual abuse, a proliferation of churches and religious centers, and abuse of religion are becoming the norm. A great part of our world has made immense progress in science, technology, medicine, and other branches of learning and has raised the standard of living, increased the comforts of life, and lengthened life expectancy. But mankind's socio-ethical conscience, moral development, and spiritual development have not kept pace with their material improvement. In fact, humanity has become more selfish and less inclined to take compassion on their less fortunate neighbors, the poor, the needy, and the oppressed. Mankind has made very minute progress in his effort to bring an end to division, disharmony, and violence.

While this work discusses the Nigerian Civil War (1967–1970) as well as other wars and violence around the globe, it also insists that we do not forget nor cease to learn from that horrible inhumanity to fellow humans, the Holocaust of 1939–1945, in which the Jews suffered untold tortures under Hitler, during which more than 6,000,000 Jews lost their lives.

The holocaust is not a fictional event. In 2014 I led a pilgrimage to Poland, during which we traced the footsteps of Saints Faustina, Maximillian Kolbe, and John Paul II. As part of our journey, we visited Auschwitz and Birkinau concentration camp. It was sorrowful to witness this painful remnant of "man's inhumanity to man."

Each day in our lives, God's spirit enables us to defend the truth and embrace our crosses. God's spirit also prepares us with answers and explanations for "anyone who ask us for reason for our hope" (1 Pet 3:15-18).

It enables us to condemn what Hitler did to the Jews. It brings hope wherever there is despair, joy in place of sadness, patience when we are tempted to act impatiently, and unity when there is division. The type of savagery human beings imposed upon their fellow human beings in recent history is not easily obliterated from memory. We cannot forget the racism in Europe and the United States of America and apartheid in South Africa in recent history. What of the Gulf War, the Liberian crisis, and the tension in Angola, Iraq, Somalia, Sierra Leone, Syria, Georgia, and Venezuela?

The Nigerian Civil War grew out of the long and still elusive search for unity between northern and southern Nigerians. The ugly experiences of this war are still evident in all sectors of life. Politically, northern and southern Nigeria have been battlefields of tribal interest and selfish motivations. The situation is marked by acute ethnicity, disunity, political instability, violence, religious fanaticism, and corruption of all kinds—as mentioned in my first work, *Corruption in Nigerian Culture: The Liberating Mission of the Church* (1994). This present work builds on this and expands our discussion on the subject of corruption in light of the morality tale in the book of Judges.

In addition to its discussion of corruption, this work alarms us of the ongoing insecurity, injustice, oppression, kidnappings, terrorism, crimes, fear, unemployment, human degradation, and the rising tide of atheistic secularism in Nigeria. Economically, Nigeria is a nation of the survival of the fittest. The gap between the rich and the poor, the haves and have-nots, is widening as I write and as you read. Hunger, hardship, and suffering are boldly written on the foreheads of fellow Nigerians, while wealth, power, excess, and waste are colorfully displayed on the "very few fellow Nigerians."

Religion cannot claim innocence. The entire world is familiar with the ongoing divide between the Muslim-north and the Christian-south. We are equally aware of the dichotomy among Muslim sects and Christian denominations themselves.

In Nigerian domestic life, broken homes and infidelity are on the rise. This disharmony spreads, affecting everything from schools to institutions, the armed forces, and trade unions. In other words, Nigerian-north and Nigerian-south are still searching for unity and peaceful coexistence.

In light of what has been described, this work aims primarily to present those factors responsible for the endless search for ethics and unity. It also aims to suggest possible solutions—or at least encourages us to rethink human behavior and how we treat one another, irrespective of class, culture, religion, gender, color, tribes, political parties, or race.

Uniquely, unlike the first edition, this edition is divided into seven chapters. Chapter one addresses unlimited social factors, including loss of family values as fundamentally contributing factors to disunity in the society today. In chapter two, we address this topic from the perspective of religions. Chapter three identifies abuse of politics and political power as contributing factors to the instability and dysfunctionality experienced in today's society. Chapter four sums up the nucleus of the first edition, which was on the abuse of mass media. It argues that mass media could help in building or rebuilding and disuniting Nigeria or any given society. Its effects, positive or negative, depend on how it is used.

The remaining three chapters (5, 6, and 7) are arranged according to what I call "biblical theology of unity"—that is, a theology that stresses unity, harmony, universalism, or avoidance of conflict, division, exclusivism, and particularism from a Judeo-Christian context.[1]

Thankfully, Scripture includes numerous biblical narratives alluding to conflict, splits, particularism, and the testing of unity. These passages, some of which I have simply and broadly cited include the Genesis accounts of Adam and Eve's relationship with God (Gen 1–3), Cain and Abel (Gen 4–5), Noah (Gen 6–11), Abraham and Lot (Gen 13–14), Esau and Jacob (Gen 28:5–22), and Joseph and his brothers (Gen 37–50). Scripture, some of which I have also intentionally mentioned in passing presents many passages having to do with unity, particularly in the New Testament Gospels and Pauline writings.

In biblical history, division and particularism existed side by side with the increasing and rightful urge for unity and universalism. This is true during the period of Judges and of the monarchy, supported by election theology and monotheism, two major features of Judaism.[2] Division is also well pronounced in the split between northern and southern Israel. Ten

---

1. I narrowly use "particularism" and "universalism" here in light of the "doctrine of universal salvation or redemption" and of "grace limited to a particular group" discussed in Park, *Either Jew or Gentile*, 9–12.

2. Park, *Either Jew or Gentile*, 12.

tribes, led by Jeroboam, went to the north, while two went to the south, led by king Rehoboam.

It was not until the time of Isaiah of Babylon, usually called Deutero-Isaiah, that we hear the strong voice of a new hermeneutics of election and monotheism in the form of a universal God, as we see in the metaphorical expression "light to the nations" (Isa 42:6; 49:6). In his new hermeneutics, Isaiah of Babylon established that the people of Israel were chosen so that they, too, can be God's instrument of salvation for all: Jews and Gentiles, rich and poor, male and female, blacks and whites, immigrant or citizen.

After the Babylonian Exile, Isaiah's position was in tension with that of Ezra and Nehemiah (Ezra 9:1–10; Neh 13:23–3), who called Jews to divorce the foreign women they had married in exile. The "unity view" of Isaiah of Babylon is supported throughout Scripture, not only by the narrative of Jonah and Ruth but by the New Testament theology concerning the universal and salvific events of Christ's life and values. [3]

Since many have already discussed these events and the biblical theology of unity, conflict and peace, division and unity, and particularism and universalism, chapter five is strictly dedicated to a reflection on one of the causes of conflict and disunity in our society today—namely, corruption. [4] This is done using the morality tale in Judges 17:1–6 as a case study.

Chapter six follows up with an intertextual study of Isaiah 40:4–5 and Luke 3:4–6 stressing the need for the church—especially the church in Africa—to open her doors and welcome and witness the gospel to everyone.

Finally, chapter seven heightens our argument for unity among everyone, the "weak" and the "strong," from the perspectives of Romans 14 and 15.

Although each chapter has a brief summary or conclusion, a major conclusion is drawn at the end. This conclusion insists on dialogue, forgiveness, prudence, tolerance, harmony, unity, inclusivity, universalism, prayer, and self-control. It also insists on the need for everyone to recognize the importance and urgency of being our brothers' and sisters' keepers in imitation of Christ and his values.

In sum, this work discusses the issues of conflict, friction, and disunity in the world—and in Nigeria in particular—from a biblical, historical, and sociocultural perspective. These issues are endemic not only in the

---

3. Ibid., 13–14.

4. Some of these works include those of Dempsey and Shapiro (eds.), *Transforming Conflict*; Park, *Either Jew or Gentile*.

economic and political structures of Nigerian society, but also in her social and religious fabric, traceable to the family as the foundation of any given society. These societal ills are found in religious groups and the political elite, as well as among journalists and the media. This work singles out materialism, infidelity, relativism, fundamentalism, ethnocentrism, anthropocentrism, ignorance, bribery, corruption, and other forms of injustice as contributory factors. Drawing broadly from biblical examples, it argues for prayer, proper education, truth-telling, restoration of family values, inter-religious and cultural dialogue, ecumenism, the enforcement of rule of law, and faith and trust in God as a way out from the conflict, violence, friction, and disunity in our contemporary society.

1

Social Power of the Family and Unity

CHARITY BEGINS AT HOME. I would like to begin with Nigeria, my country of birth and the giant of Africa. Nigeria, like other nations, is increasingly searching for harmony and oneness. This national experience is traceable to the family, which is a group of people who are descendants of a common ancestor.[1] The family is the basic or fundamental unit of social organization. It is the primary vital cell of society.[2] A family is the first and fundamental school of social living.[3] It is a place where different generations come together and help one another to grow wisely, maturely, and prudently and harmonize the rights of individuals with other demands of social life.

The family remains the primordial community. As the font of new human life, it is the normal, if not the only, center in which the human person can develop bodily and spiritually in a healthy fashion.[4] The moral, political, economic, and religious life of our children and their ability to love is first awakened by parental love and formation. That is to say that the family propagates the race and helps to stem the tide of social order.

A good nation begins from the family. The United Nations begins from a united and stable family. Through the family as its cell, backbone,

---

1. *Advanced Learner's Dictionary*, 308.

2. *Apostolicam Actuositatem*, no.11.

3. *Familiaris Consortio*, no. 37.

4. Peschke, *Christian Ethics*, 242.

7

and bedrock, our contemporary society everywhere maintains and renews itself. Chukwuma Francis is on points when he says;

> The family is the backbone as well as the bedrock of the society. This belief arises from the fact that the people who make up society are born and nurtured in the family during their early years. The family is an indispensable part of the society, especially for its continuity. It feeds the society with its fundamental constituents, human beings. The family and the larger society are so linked up that any progress or defect in one automatically reflects in the other. If the family gets forlorn or broken, then the peaceful continuity of the society is on fire, for serious damage.[5]

When we observe global families today, we see that Chukwumu's assertion is not far from the truth. Most defects and damages we notice in Nigerian families today, both in the north and the south, reflect the social and public life of the nation and the world at large.

It is through the family as its cell that society maintains, unites, and renews itself. Vatican Council II rightly exhorts that the "well-being of the individual person and of both human and Christian society is closely bound up with the healthy state of conjugal and family life."[6] Therefore, the restoration of a united and just society constantly begins with the renewal of the family.

It is in the renewed family that its economical, educational, protective, and recreational functions and responsibilities are fulfilled. As an economic unit, the family provides for food, shelter, and clothing. As an educational background, the intellectual, moral, and social development of the human person is realized. Moreover, the importance of education in fostering orderliness, peace, and understanding cannot be overemphasized.

In the family, youth and young Nigerians earnestly receive their primordial knowledge of the ethics of the world around them. They are first taught the unselfishness of mutual love and coexistence. Put simply, the two most social virtues of charity and justice are taught in the family. Besides charity and social justice, the excellent virtues of obedience, modesty, just rule, and respect to human dignity with rights are cultivated in the family.

Until parents learn how to lead justly and exemplarily in the family, they are not in a position to give a harmonized authority and service in public life. This is true especially with a public service compatible with the

5. Chukwumu, "Broken Families," 24.

6. *Gaudium et spes*, no. 47.

8

dignity, joy, peace, and rights of the human person. The desired readiness to help, consideration of others, fairness, transparent sincerity, brotherliness, leadership by example, patriotism, and diligence needed for a fruitful search for unity in Nigeria and other nations must have their solid foundations laid in the family. Children with brothers and sisters learn from the very beginning to control themselves, to share with others, to claim no more rights than others, to be obliging, and to be self-sacrificing, available, and loyal. A family with a sound spirit of oneness and prayer brings an educative influence to bear on the parents who are obliged to put forth their best selves in order to achieve fully a happy family and nation.

Furthermore, as a spiritual home for its members, they find in their daily living based on love, trust esteem, and respect. There is also an exchange of ideas, convictions, values, and attitudes, a sharing of the experiences of joys, sorrows, successes, and trials.[7] In other words, the much needed and desired family unity and proper home training is not yet fully found in the present day Nigerian society and beyond. In fact, ours is a state of moral infancy, divorce, polygamy, broken homes, worship of money, frivolous court litigation, materialism, divination of sex, and disunity. In other words, the situation in modern society is very challenging as adults have failed to set good examples for the younger generations. Their record-breaking rate of marital infidelity, family rifts, division, divorce, worship of money, and gross indiscipline have been marring progress in society at large. One wonders what factors are responsible.

FACTORS RESPONSIBLE FOR DIVIDED HOMES AND FAMILIES

There are many factors responsible for broken homes and families all over the world, and in Nigeria in particular. Some of these factors require some brief comment, including the unlimited and inordinate pursuit for wealth, material things, and freedom, infidelity, drunkenness, impatience, refusal to seek reconciliation, infertility, and childlessness.

The human person is a composite being. People are made up of body and soul, matter and form. The material needs, as well as spiritual needs, are necessary for a balanced human person. But an overemphasis on one to the detriment of the other is not good. This seems to be the case in our modern world. Many families both within and outside Nigeria have to work

7. David, "Marriage," 43.

or keep two to three jobs to make ends meet. In some areas, this requires a balancing act. Wives and husbands are found inordinately pursuing material things to the detriment of their family's unity.

Divorced couples have told me that they wanted to have freedom. Their view of freedom seemed to include the sense of being independent, owning personal homes, operating personal bank accounts, driving personal cars, not been talked over, acting according to their desires, and traveling at will. In other words, they did not want to answer to anyone.

Additionally, many in our society today have not been able to keep to their marriage and vocational promises of fidelity. Some parents have even turned into "sugar daddies" and "sugar–mummies," engaging in extramarital relations with youth of the same age as their sons and daughters. Cheating on one's partner, apart from leading to home destruction and the breakdown of family trust, is an offense against God and his commandments. It is also an immoral act unacceptable in most religious and cultural societies.

Drunkenness is another identifiable factor responsible for the breakdown of the family. Any married partner who has unfortunately formed the bad habit of excessive drinking would eventually end up neglecting his family responsibilities. This naturally leads to a disorganized and broken family.

Impatience and the refusal to seek reconciliation when offended have also been identified as negative factors. Many are extremely fast to react revengefully to their partner's shortcomings. Where patience, endurance, tolerance, and a spirit of forgiveness are lacking, disunity is bound to reign, and often this spreads into public offices and nation capitals.

Unfortunately, infertility and childlessness in many environments and cultures are serious issues. Traditionally, couples without children in African culture are not only subjects of ridicule and laughter, but like the biblical Sarah (Gen 11:30) and other matriarchs, they are regarded as a curse. Moreover, differences in temperament, search for male issues, religious beliefs, and poverty can also contribute to family disharmony, which most often matures or spreads into a national social disharmony prevalent in the world today, especially in Nigeria.

SOCIAL DISHARMONY BEYOND NIGERIA:
A REAPPRAISAL

Nigerians as well as citizens of many other nations are ever in search for that illusive social understanding and harmony traceable to the family root. Socially, Nigeria is a society where the poor are assisted to become poorer. Justice and honesty have become subjects of laughter. By justice here we mean: "How wealth, power, privileges, rights and responsibilities are distributed to every level—local, natural, and global.[8] Door's thoughts on social or distributive justice may be useful here. For Door, "justice is vital for all generations and groups . . . it's important and an indispensable moral concept for a healthy society."[9]

Historically, justice has been seen as indispensable in any society. This was true of Cepahalus. He saw justice as the speaking of the truth and payment of one's debt, while his contemporary Thrasymcus understood justice as the interest of the ruler.[10] Plato defined it as a virtue whose fundamental nature and structure was as much in the life of an individual as in the way in which a society is organized; that is why he believed that "the just man is the one whom part of the soul is harmoniously governed by reason."[11] Aristotle conceived of justice as the greatest virtue whereby one does the right thing, believing in the right conduct, wishing what is right, and wishing above all, the law should be maintained while treating equals equally.[12]

St. Augustine was among several other scholastic philosophers who championed the crusade against immorality and injustice that may interest today's society. Augustine saw justice as "the habit of the soul, which impart to everyman the dignity due to him."[13] St. Thomas Aquinas, on the other hand, defined justice as "a habit whereby a man renders to each one his due by constant and perpetual will." [14]

One of the most remarkable modern philosophers to raise the issue of justice was David Hume (1711–1776). As an empiricist, the central fact about ethics for Hume is that moral judgements are formed not by reason

8. Door, *Spirituality and Justice*, 14.

9. Udoekpo, *Worship in Amos*, 105.

10. Cf. Plato, *Republic*, 73–74.

11. Ibid., 74.

12. Stumph, *Philosophy*, 156–157.

13. Ibid., 57.

14. Aquinas, *Summa Theologica*, 1429.

alone but by the sentiment of sympathy. He argues that justice, which he describes as "general peace and order" or "a general abstinence from the possession of others," reflects the self-interest of each person who desires to be secured in person and property. This security and happiness can be achieved only in society, in an arrangement of justice. To this extent, justice is a reflection of self-interest. The usefulness of justice is that it satisfies self-interest. In other words, "self-interest is the original motive to the establishment of justice; but a sympathy with public interest is the source of the moral approbation which attends that virtue.[15]

Benedict Spinoza, a Dutch-Jewish philosopher, also spoke to us indirectly by considering justice as "the habitual rendering to everyman his lawful due, is justice, while injustice is depriving a man, under the pretense of legality of that the laws rightly interpreted would allow him."[16] Thomas Hobbes maintained that "'just' and 'unjust' presupposes obligations and that no complaint of injustice could be made against the sovereign legislator." [17] Finally, a Nigerian author describes justice as "the concrete accomplishments of the fundamental imperative which calls for positive respect for the dignity and rights of others and contribution of the meeting of human necessity."[18]

In all, the preceding reviews of the meaning of justice have often led to the classification of justice into: "commutative" (advocating for a fair stand of giving and receiving what is assigned to a person); "distributive" (classification of goods and resources equally and fairly to all); "retributive" (having as its ends and finality correction, restoration, and restitution of offences and damages done); and "social justice," which is a simply seen as a general justice requiring general good in all its aspects with regard to the needs of everyone in the society, poor and rich.[19]

Nicholas Wolterstorff's *Justice, right and wrong* (2008) is one of the most impressive works on justice since John Rawls' *Theory of Justice*, who basically emphasized equal respect for all members of the social order

---

15. See Stumph, *Philosophy*, 299; Udoekpo, *Concept of Unen*, 4–5; Udoekpo, unpublished work "Annang & Judeo-Christian," 3–5.

16. Spinoza, *Theologico-Political Treatise*, 208.

17. Benn, "Justice," 298.

18. John, "Justice and Peace," 1.

19. Udoekpo, *Unen*, 10–17; Udoekpo, unpublished work "Annang & Judeo-Christian," 3–5.

"as moral persons."[20] Wolterstorff not only acknowledges the distinction between distributive, commutative, rectifying, and corrective justice, but defines justice in light of St. John Chrysostom as inherent natural rights superior to mere just a right order. [21] Wolterstorff is mostly interested in distributive justice, or what he calls "primary justice." For him, rectifying justice "consists of the justice that becomes relevant when there was a breakdown in the distributive and commutative justice."[22]

He arrived at his notion of primary or distributive justice as an inherent right to all human beings (not just as the mere platonic "right order") by reading the definition of justice found in the Justinian's *Digest*, a codification of the Roman law. The *Digest* begins with the third-century Roman jurist Ulpian's famous definition of justice as "a steady and enduring will to render to each their *ius*."[23] Although Ulpian's emphasis was on possession of right and the virtue of justice, Wolterstorff's emphasis is on the "social condition that those who possess the virtue seek to bring about."[24]

Similarly, generations of Nigerians and global citizens in various settings—whether in politics, religion, culture, ownership, possession, economics, family, relationship, farming, fishing, hunting, or commerce—have always had a profound and natural sense of right and wrong, good and bad, as well as a deep sense of concern for justice. This concern for justice is currently lacking in Nigeria and in other political capitals throughout the world.

Ours situation today is one where wealth, power, privilege, rights, and responsibilities are not justly distributed to all levels of people. Ours is also a society whereby the poor remain poor, while the rich progress no matter how immoral the means may be. There seems to be no hope for the common person, no hope for the minority and the "weaponless" in different parts of the world. With regard to power and sociopolitical and economic authorities, there is an attitude of indifference to the poor or a complete lack of compassion and sentiments of brotherliness, love, and unity. Pope Francis currently challenges this situation. He calls us to reject an economy that excludes the poor—to reject capitalism, individualism, relativism,

---

20. Rawls, *Theory of Justice*, 447.

21. See Chrysostom's work on *Wealth and Poverty*.

22. Wolsterstorff, *Justice, Rights and Wrongs*, ix.

23. Ibid., 22.

24. Ibid., 22–23.

fundamentalism, the idolatry of money, and a financial system that rules rather than serves. He calls us to reject the inequality that spawns violence.[25]

In Nigeria and in other parts of the world there is no denying that in addition to what Francis has warned against, political cliques and religious denominations exist. The majority and the minority of the people are both unnecessarily tribe conscious, such that national daily activities are painted with impressionable brushes such as: "Where is he from?" "Is he a northerner or a southerner, a Christian or a Muslim?" "Is he a Catholic or a Protestant?" In Europe and in the United States of America we would call it racism and segregation.

Lamenting the dysfunctional and destabilizing existence of tribalism, unhealthy boundaries, unnecessary walls, and social division persistent in Nigeria, Michael Edem, a Vincentian Clergy, once wrote;

> Socially, Nigeria is propelled by the philosophy of Conglomerationism, groupism, gathering together or bonding together or drawing together for a particular purpose, what the Psychologists call mob or group psychology.[26]

Today, the emphasis seems to be on where and which group one belongs, to the detriment of the weak, whom St. Paul addresses in Romans 14–15 (see the last chapter of this work). [27] Nigeria is a nation where the famous biblical story of the social oppression of God's chosen people in Israel has repeated itself in an acute but modern fashion.

Some of the passages in the biblical story are worth revisiting for the sake of our contemporary society. The legislative texts, prophetic literature, psalms, historical books, and wisdom literature of ancient Israel express great concern for social justice. Let us first examine the legislative texts. In the law codes (Exod 20:22–23:33, Lev; Deut 17–26), such as Exodus 22:21 and 23:9, justice is understood as treating the widow, the sojourner, and the fatherless fairly. The ancient Israelites understood justice as loving sojourners and seeing them as one of themselves (Lev 19:33–34; Deut 10:19).[28]

Bruce Malchow is right in noticing that Leviticus 24:22 further specifies that sojourners and natives are to be governed by one law.

25. See Pope Francis, *Evangeli Gaudium*, nos. 51–75; Udoekpo, *Israel's Prophets*, 81–87.

26. Edem, *Confused Values*, 33.

27. This reflection was once shared with the *Mustard Seed Magazine* of the Catholic Institute of West Africa, Port Harcourt, Nigeria.

28. Udoekpo, "Annang and Judeo-Christian," 11.

These commands reveal high ethical sensitivity in not only providing total justice for people easily misused but also in calling for equality and love toward them. In Leviticus 22:26 we see what the ancient Israelites think of the justice of pledges and material objects given as collateral for loans. They "insists that garments given in pledge are to be returned before sundown. Without a cloak a poor person would have no covering for the night."[29]

Also, in ancient Israel, laws were constantly renewed and updated or interpreted with reference to others. For example, the idea expressed in Leviticus 22 is extended in Deuteronomy 24:17. This text prohibits the use of a widow's garment as a pledge. A creditor is forbidden from going into a debtor's apartment to fetch a pledge (Deut 24:10–11). The laws on interest protect the deprived and the marginalized. Collecting interest from the poor who borrow is seen as unjust (Exod 22:25). This sense of justice is expanded in Leviticus 23:19–20. The use of false weights or measures was regarded as unjust behavior (Deut 25:13–15). The poor and hired servants must be paid the wages due to them (Deut 24:1–15). Rich farmers were to allow the poor and widows to glean in their fields (Deut 24:19–22; Lev 19:9–10; 23:22; cf. Ruth).

Wolterstorff timely and indirectly signals to us that in the midst of a lengthy catalogue of legislative materials of Israel's life, Moses's exhortation that follows is worth reflectively re-reading:

> You shall appoint judges and officials throughout your tribes, in all your towns that the Lord your God is giving you, and they shall render just decision for the people. You must not distort justice; you must not show partiality; and you must not accept bribes, for a bribe blinds the eyes of the wise and subverts the cause of those who are in the right. Justice, and only justice, you shall pursue, so that you may live and occupy the land that the Lord your God is giving you. (Deut 16:18–20)[30]

In this context, I agree with Wolsterstorff that what lay behind the injunctions of Amos and other Israelite prophets (especially Micah, Isaiah, and Jeremiah) on matters of justice was their conviction that the people were not following the demands for justice in the legislative texts, including Deuteronomy 16:18–20.[31]

---

29. Malchow, *Social Justice*, 23.

30. See Wolsterstorff, *Justice, Right and Wrongs*, 70.

31. Ibid., 70–71.

God commissioned Amos, a wealthy man from Tekoa (a town in Judah south of Jerusalem), as a prophet to challenge injustice in the northern kingdom of Israel. In Amos 5 the prophet Amos says, "Ah, you that turn justice (*mišpaṭ*) to wormwood, and bring righteousness (*tsədāqâ*) to the ground!"(Amos 5:7 *NRSV*). Wormwood was a dwarf bitter shrub. Amos' listeners, like some of us in modern society, must have broken the dictates of the legislative texts, and were changing the sweetness of justice to the bitterness of injustice.[32]

O'Donovan puts it so well, saying, "When Amos calls for *mišpaṭ* (justice) to roll down like waters and righteousness (*tsədāqâ*) like ever-flowing stream (v. 24), he means precisely that the stream of juridical activity should not be allowed to dry up."[33] On another occasion Amos addresses wives of the corrupt elite as "Cows of Bashan who are on Mount Samaria, who oppress the poor, who crush the needy, who say to their husbands, 'bring something to drink' "(Amos 4:1). Amos was not out to please the First Ladies, as we sometimes do in modern politics; nor was he intending to please their elite husbands and courts officials. His motive was to defend justice.[34]

Defending justice against court officials in the Jerusalem temple, Micah, another Israelite prophet worthy of listening to and learning from, says,

> Listen, you heads of Jacobs, and rulers of the house of Israel!
> Should you not know justice?—you who hate the good and love the evil, who tear the skin off my people, and he flesh off their bones; who eat the flesh of my people, fly their skin off them, break their bones in pieces, and chop them up like meant in a kettle, like flesh in a caldron. (Mic 3:1–3)

In chapter 7 Micah reiterates, "the official and the judge ask for a bribe, and the powerful dictate what they desire; thus they pervert justice" (Mic 7:3). His contemporary, Isaiah of Jerusalem, calls the people to "learn to do good; seek justice, rescue the oppressed, defend the orphan, and plead for the widow" (Isa 1:17; cf. 59:4). He also speaks of those "who cause a person to lose a lawsuit, who set a trap for the arbiter in the gate, and without grounds deny justice to the one in the right" (Isa 29:21).

---

32. Malchow, *Social Justice*, 34; Udoekpo, *Worship in Amos*, 84.

33. O'Donovan, *Desires of the Nations*, 41–42.

34. Malchow, *Social Justice*, 35; Udoekpo, *Worship in Amos*, 107.

Similarly, Jeremiah, who witnessed the temple of Jerusalem inflamed, attacks Jehoiakim for doing the opposite of justice:

> Woe to him who builds his house by unrighteousness, and his upper rooms by injustice; who makes his neighbors work for nothing, and does not give them their wages; . . . Are you a king because you compete in cedar? Did you father eat and drink and do justice and righteousness? (Jer 22:13–17)

Jehoiakim's use of forced labor (as Solomon before him did) to renovate his old palace did not sit well with Jeremiah. He pointed out that Jehoiakim was not following in the footsteps of his father, Josiah, who fulfilled the ideal of kingship by rightly judging the needy. Comparably, Isaiah of Babylon says that "no one brings suit justly, no one goes to law honestly; they rely on empty pleas, they speak lies, conceiving mischief and begetting iniquity" (Isa 59:4).

Like the prophetic books, some passages in the psalms communicate a concern for justice that can serve as a lesson for us today in Nigeria and beyond. Psalm 10, for instance, imagines the thought process of the oppressors thus:

> In the pride of their countenance the wicked say, "God will not seek it out"; all their thoughts are, "There is not God." Their ways prosper at all times; your judgements are on high, out of their sight; as for their foes, they scoff at them. They think in their heart, "We shall not be moved; throughout all generations we shall not met adversity." (Ps 10:4–6)

Also, the oppressors,

> Sit in ambush in the villages; in hiding places they murder the innocent. Their eyes stealthily watch for the helpless; they lurk in secret like a lion in its covert; they lurk that they may seize the poor; they seize the poor and drag them off in their net and the helpless fall by their might. (Ps 10:8–10)

In Psalm 10:12–15 the psalmist, with the spirit of social inversion, invites God to intervene: "Rise up, O Lord; O God, lift up your hand; do not forget the oppressed. Why do the wicked renounce God and say in their hearts, 'You will not call us to account'? . . . Break the arm of the wicket and evildoers; seek out their wickedness until you find none."[35]

---

35. Brueggemann, "Psalms 9–10," 11.

In light of these encouraging verses of the Bible, and in the midst of the challenges of disunity and injustice we face around the globe, and in Africa in particular, other passages in Scripture talk about justice and righteousness as the very foundation of God's throne. Psalm 89 says:

> Let the heavens praise you wonders, O Lord, your faithfulness in the assembly of the holy ones. For who in the skies can be compared to the Lord? Who among the heavenly beings is like the Lord . . . ? The heavens are yours, the earth also is yours; . . . Righteousness and justice are the foundation of your thrones; steadfast love and faithfulness go before you. (Ps 89:5–14)

Psalm 33 also links justice to God's very act of creation: "[God] loves righteousness and justice; the earth is full of the steadfast love of the Lord" (Ps 33:5). Yoder argues that, in light of Psalm 33 and Psalm 89, and many others, "God as God of justice is connected with God as the creator of the world. "[36]

The psalmists in a few other places also talk about oppressors killing the needy in Israel: "They crush your people, O Lord, and afflict your heritage. They kill the widow and the stranger, they murder the orphan" (Ps 94:5–6). We can conclude that the psalmists add to Israel's legacy for social justice. By the content of their prayers, they appealed for those who were enduring crises. They advocated for justice. They championed righteousness. They also reinterpreted legislative texts and added to past traditions new forms of expressing confidence in the love of God to assist the poor and the victims of injustice.[37] This is the limit of what we need for unity to exist and endure in our society today.

In the historical books, especially in the Deuteronomic and Chronicler's histories, including Ruth and Ezra-Nehemiah, we also find references to justice and righteousness as sources of peace and unity. For example, we hear echoes of social justice in 1 Samuel 2:1–10. Reflecting Mary's Magnificat in Luke's Gospel, 1 Samuel's passage reads:

> The bows of the mighty are broken, but the feeble gird on strength. Those who were full have hired themselves out for bread, but those who were hungry have ceased to hunger forever. . . The Lord makes poor and makes rich; he brings low, he also exalts. He raises up the poor from the dust; he lifts the needy from the ash heap, to make them sit with princes and inherit a seat of honor. (1 Sam 2:4–8)

36. Yoder, *Shalom*, 26.

37. Mlachow, *Social Justice*, 57.

A similar message of justice is heard in the prophet Nathan's parable to David (2 Sam 12:1–4), the passages recounting the charity showed to Elijah the prophet (1 Kgs 17:8–16), the story of Naboth's vineyard (1 Kgs 21), and the story of Ruth, Naomi, and Boaz (Ruth 2:1–11).

Justice is also emphasized in the narrative where King Jehoshaphat appointed judges in 2 Chronicles 19:5–7:

> Consider what you are doing, for you judge not on behalf of human beings but on the Lord's behalf; he is with you in giving judgment. Now let the fear of the Lord be upon you; take care what you do, for there is no perversion of justice with the Lord our God, or partiality, or taking of bribes.

Justice is also emphasized in the memoirs of Nehemiah (Neh 5:1–13). In this text, the wealthy seemed to have forced the poor to surrender some of their property as well as enslaved their children and grandchildren. Nehemiah is a good example of a wealthy man, like Amos and others, who side with and advocate for the poor. They challenge the wealthy businessmen and women of today to unite in solidarity with the poor and the needy of our society.

We also hear echoes of justice and righteousness, ingredients for unity, in some passages of wisdom literature (Proverbs, Job, Ecclesiastes, Sirach, and Wisdom). The wisdom literature of Scripture draws on concepts we see in other Near Eastern wisdom texts. Comments on them are not within the scope of this work. Although the wisdom texts possess prophetic influence, they emphasize fear of the Lord, prudence, the need to keep the Torah, elegance, faith, self-control, justice, and good attitudes toward wealth, as well as charity (Prov 28:27; Job 31:16–20).

In regard to wealth, Scripture acknowledges the common human beliefs that "money answers everything" (Eccl 10:19), the rich rule the poor (Prov 22:7), wealth is a rich person's rotection (Prov 10:15), wealth brings honor (Prov 10:30–31), and the rich are surrounded by friends while the poor are isolated (Prov 14:20; 19:4; Sir 13:21–22). But in contrast to these perceptions, Scripture offers the wise counsel that God is not only the source of wealth, but he is the one who gives the power to enjoy wealth (Eccl 5:18–19). Things greater than ordinary wealth include wisdom (Prov 3:13–15), tranquility (Prov 17:1), a good name (Prov 22:1), health (Sir 30:14–16), fear of the Lord, and love as sources of unity (Prov 15:16–17).

Additionally, it is wise to respect the poor and the needy. Proverbs 30:13–14 warns of the proud who devour the poor like cannibals.

Wisdom 2:10–11 cautions the ungodly who plan to oppress the poor and the widow and the risks of claiming that might makes right.

In sum, in wisdom literature, like other Old Testament passages, we find the defense of the poor as well as the promotion of justice, peace, and unity in Israel.

To end this biblical review on justice as a key to unity, we must offer a word or two on the New Testament. Although chapter six is dedicated to Luke and Isaiah of Babylon's teachings in regard to unity, we will briefly add that Luke-Acts mention a number of underclass voices in Jewish society. For instance, these books mention Zechariah, a minor priest; two hill-country women, both pregnant, Elizabeth, the elderly wife of Zechariah, and Mary, a young relative of Elizabeth; Simeon, a pious elderly Jerusalemite; Ann, an extremely pious eighty-four-year-old widow; and some shepherds. And what they said came to a fulfilment. Luke presents his narratives as the continuation of a story already told.[38] It is a story of salvation history (*heilsgeschichte*), divine necessity, and justice already told in the Old Testament. Affirming this in his *Moral Vision of the New Testament*, Richard Hays say,

> The Gospel of Luke and Acts of the Apostles are two parts of a single grand literary work in which Luke tells the story of salvation history in a stately and gracious manner. God's mighty act of deliverance through Jesus Christ is narrated as an epic, in such a way that the church might discover its location in human history, particularly within the history of God's dealings with his people Israel.[39]

Hays rightly notes that the story offered by Luke the historian is not just an empty story, but a story of God's justice that leads to peace and unity. In Luke, as we shall find more in chapter six, Jesus is the one who brings justice and unity to God's people—the poor and the rich, the blind and the captives—as evidenced in the scroll that reads;

> the spirit of the Lord is upon me, because he has anointed me to bring good news to the poor; He sent me to proclaim release to the captives and recovery of sight to the blind, to let the oppressed to go free, to proclaim the year of the Lord's favor. (Luke 4:17–21; cf. Isa 61:1–2)

---

38. Matera, *New Testament Theology*, 52–55.

39. Hays, *Moral Vision*, 112.

This is the same theme of rectifying justice that we heard in Luke 1:46–53, when Mary our Mother prays,

> My soul magnifies the Lord, and my spirit rejoices in God my savior, for he has looked with favor on the lowliness of his server . . . He has brought down the powerful from their thrones, and lifted up the lowly; he has filled the hungry with good things, and sent the rich away empty. (Luke 1:46–53)

The theme of justice or of social inversion, which is much needed in society today, is equally heard in the lowly shepherds, who were elevated by the message of the heavenly good news that to the city of David will be born this day a Savior (Luke 2:10–11). The New Testament vision of justice (cf. Luke 18:1–8; 23:26–43; Matt 23:1–36), which is drawn, adapted, contextualized, and reinterpreted from the Old Testament texts we reviewed above, can be described as assertive, inclusive, and reconciling.[40]

These biblical views of justice and righteousness as sources of peace, unity, harmony, inclusiveness, and a sense of universalism remain consoling in spite of the seeming darkness of the present-day Nigeria. It is not sufficient to shout from a golden and excessively furnished government apartment, "One Nigeria, this country belongs to all!" when one's practical attitude is that of "eliminate the Infidels and the weak!"

Nigeria has yet to become a country of the people, where tribal leaders, racism, sectionalism, segregation, coups, and coup-mates are nonexistent. Nigeria and other countries have not yet become places that prioritize the desired sense of common goals, justice, and duty over color, tribal marks, language, or dialect.

Michael Edem reinforces this point in his valuable book *Confused Values in Nigeria: Rituals Reveal Mythology*. He argues:

> They will say so many lofty and beautiful things about Nigeria, but will not lift a finger to implement. Such people are very much at home with their language. Their language is used as a barrier to cut off others. Even transaction is carried out in their language. The so called Lingua-Franca-English is thrown away as garbage. One who does not speak or understand the language is at a loss. It happens in the offices and at conversations at family circles as well. In the offices, a non-speaker of such language cannot transact any business.[41]

40. See Dempsey, *Justice,* 36–43.
41. Edem, *Confused Values,* 34–35.

This is what divides us. This is what kills and dampens our desired unity. This is why we must pray for togetherness. Our divided social experiences are further rooted and manifested in the once celebrated "quota system" employed in Nigerian institutions and schools for admissions. This was a famous practice that was meant to help us get the best of our youth so as to catch up with other international counterparts. If the country belongs to us, if Nigeria is our home, the citizens should be given personal and individual rights based on merit, talent, and charisma. There should a place for everyone, the poor and the rich, the weak and the strong. A Nigerian in the north and a Nigerian in the south should be allowed to feel at home in schools, companies, and offices anywhere in the country. There should be a sense of common good as we have in Europe and in the United States (though not perfect).

Though chapter seven of this work is dedicated to Paul's insights on the subjects of unity, inclusiveness, justice, universalism of all, Jews and Gentiles, weak and the strong, Paul's advice to a divided and quarrelsome Corinthian community in 1 Corinthian 12 is consoling to our modern divided society. Paul says,

> There are varieties of gifts, but the same Spirit; and there are varieties of services, but the same Lord; and there are varieties of activities, but it is the same God who activates all of them in everyone. To each is given the manifestation of the Spirit for the common good. To one is given through the Spirit the utterance of wisdom, and to another the utterance of knowledge according to the same Spirit, to another the working of miracles, to another prophecy . . . to each one individually just as the Spirit chooses. (1 Cor 12:4–11)

This text implies, at least partly, that in Nigeria, some people could best serve as cattle tenders, farmers, medical experts, and administrators. Others can happily serve as educators, men and women in uniform, and in many other capacities. Each citizen, therefore, should in the spirit of justice be given a fair chance to freely exercise his or her gifts, talents, and contributions toward the common good of the nation.

SUMMARY

Before we examine disharmonious religious factors and their limits, we can summarize that the social factor that is traceable to family is responsible for disharmony in Nigeria. Most families experience disunity for several reasons, including acts of infidelity to partners, childlessness, wrestling with organized and societal injustices condemned in the discussed biblical history, as well as the limitless search for material things, lack of patience and endurance, incessant and unlimited habitual drunkenness, and a total lack of self-control. Therefore, since statements with false premises lead to a false conclusion, false family set-ups contribute immensely to the present false social structures in Nigeria and society at large.

2

Wars in Religious Families
and Their Limits

THIS CHAPTER, COMPLETED ON October 7, 2019, is prayerfully dedicated to Professor John S. Mbiti, a Kenyan-born and Anglican-Christian philosopher and theologian who passed away on October 6, 2019 in Switzerland. May he rest in peace! Though I did not have the privilege of meeting him in person, I thought his religious writings and theological contributions impacted many, especially in Africa. Professor Mbiti sees the complexity of religion, the subject matter of this chapter, from five perspectives: (1) beliefs; (2) practices, ceremonies, and festivals; (3) religious objects and places; (4) values and morals; and (5) religious officials and leaders.

Beliefs are an essential part of religion since they show the way we think about the universe as well as our attitude toward life as a whole. In religious practices, ceremonies, and festivals, we demonstrate our beliefs in very pragmatic and practical ways, which may include observing customs, dancing, singing, eating, and celebrating. Special places and objects are things we often need or set apart in our liturgy and religious practices. We are in various traditions conscious of certain values, including truth, justice, love, righteousness, right and wrong, good and evil, beauty, decency, respect for people, property, keeping of covenant, agreement, praise, blame, character, and integrity. Above all, in religion we have people—men and women, youth and adults—who preside at religious matters. In his view, a true definition of religion is not complete without these five components. [1]

Similarly, Richard Hess in his *Israelite Religions* recognizes the complexity of religions. He defines religion provisionally as "the service and worship of the divine or supernatural through a system of attitudes, beliefs, and practices."[2] Susan Niditch similarly confesses that when her students attempt to define religion, two headings often emerge: "the social communitarian level and personal-individual level."[3] Some see religion from the perspective of shared stories, history, values and beliefs, communal ceremonies, songs, rituals, bonds, and institutions. Others see religion from the perspective of self-development, spiritually speaking. That is, they see it as a person's special way of connecting with the supernatural through individual petitions, personal faith, or of temptation and conscience.[4]

Like Mbiti and Hess, Niditch agrees that all the above details are needed to understand religions. Borrowing from Ninian Smart's "worldview" as a better umbrella term for religion, Niditch affirms that religion has to be approached from experiential, mythical, ritual, and ethical perspectives.[5] The experiential perspective includes more direct experiences of the numinous-visions, trances, messages from God, and more subtle indications of a divine presence; the mythical perspective includes the rich, varied narrative traditions that capture and encapsulate a group's values and beliefs, their hopes and fears.[6] The ritual dimension expresses some of the same sets of symbols found in a group's myth, while the ethical dimension refers to the moral actions that guide the group.[7]

These conversations on the meaning and nature of religion among reputable scholars like John S. Mbiti, Richard Hess, Ninian Smart, Susan Niditch, and many others suggest to readers of this book how multifaceted and complex religious practices are in various traditions and settings.

In different parts of the world, especially Nigeria, religion is an incredibly divisive phenomenon. Religion contributes to our inability to coexist in our nation. The three major existing religions in Nigeria include

1. Mbiti, *African Religion*, 11–13.
2. Hess, *Israelite Religions*, 1–11.
3. Niditch, *Ancient Israelite Religion*, 3.
4. Ibid., 3.
5. Ibid., 4.
6. Ibid., 5.
7. Ibid., 5–6.

Christianity, Islam, and African Traditional Religions. These three can hardly agree all the time. One notices a very deep and transparent internal disorder and division among them.

Like Christianity and others, Islam has a very protracted and exciting history. It is not the prerogative of this work to go into that history now, but preferably to stress that disunity in the Muslim religion serves as a nursery of dichotomy in Nigeria as it is in the world over. In other words, the division in the Islamic family has an adverse social, political, and religious effect on the nation's desired togetherness. No given society is perfect. Every religious group has internal weaknesses.

Noticing this weakness in the house of Islam, Nathaniel Ndiokwere once wrote:

> There are liberals and conservatives in Islam as well as 'born again' fundamentalists and fanatics. There are mystics. Over 90% of all Moslems are said to be *Sunnis* (from '*Suna*', the tradition of the Prophets), who consider themselves to possess Islamic orthodoxy. There are also *Shi'ite* Moslems found mostly in Iran and Iraq who differ from the *Sunnis* in Islamic Theology and in their understanding of Mohammed's Successors. In Nigeria, Moslems who belong to the Shi'ite movement are portrayed as trouble makers. *Yahaya*, the so called *Shi'ite* spokesman is the leader of a radical Islamic group in Katshina, Nigeria.[8]

Ndiokwere further observes that '*Yahaya*, who claimed that his inspiration came from God, was quoted as saying that he would continue to defy all laws as far as they are made by man. In his words, "No man made law is binding on us because we do not recognize the government. The only laws we recognize are those of Allah and the Prophet Mohammed, and we are prepared to die defending them."[9] Such internal disorder and disharmony in Muslim circles between the moderate and the extremist often matures into the larger section of the society. Their beliefs, philosophy, and lack of common concept and language hamper any meaningful and constructive relationship or coexistence with other religions. This fact is conscientiously observed in the *Lineamenta* of the First African Synod, which states,

> In Africa, Islam is important and often a difficult partner in dialogue. It is an important partner because of its genuine religious values, its large followers, and the root it has struck among many

8. Ndiokwere, *African Church*, 71.

9. This was drawn from *Newswatch*, 28.

African peoples. It is a difficult partner in dialogue because of a lack of a common concept and language of dialogue. At times, its methods of conversation do raise problems for dialogue.[10]

Speaking about dialogue that is applicable to all religious groups (African Traditional Religion, Islam, and Christianity), the Bishops of the First National Pastoral Congress of Nigeria, in 1999, stressed the need for "dialogue and neighborliness." They started by invoking all parties to take seriously the need to reach to everyone, and to see this as a moral duty. They recalled the teachings of the Scriptures (1 Cor 12:11; 1 Tim 2:4) as well as those of John Paul II, who understood and taught the missionary nature (*Ad Gentes* 2) of the church to preach the gospel to the ends of the earth (Mark 16:15).[11]

The Nigerian Bishops also appealed to the teachings of the Second Vatican Council on interreligious dialogue by quoting *Nostra Aetatae* 2, which says that "the Church rejects nothing that is true and holy in the non-Christian religious which often reflect a ray of that truth which en-lightens all men."[12] What the Congress' document is referring to here in a Nigerian context are other religious groups in Nigeria apart from Christianity, especially Islam and African Traditional Religions (ATR).

While appealing to *Lumen Gentium* 6, the Congress acknowledges not only that there should be a limit to disunity, but that "Moslems profess to 'hold the faith of Abraham,' along with us adore the one merciful God . . . Though the Moslems do not acknowledge Jesus as God, they however revere Him as a prophet and also honour Mary, His Virgin Mother."[13] The Congress further draws people's attention to the fact that Muslims, like Christians, "prize the moral life, and give worship to God especially through prayer, almsgiving, and fasting."[14] We hear a similar exhortation in *Ecclesia in Africa* (*EIA*), which cautions readers not to disengage in dialogue with Islam.[15]

Additionally, *Ecclesia in Africa* recognizes the common values Africa has. These values include the spiritual view of life, respect for the dignity of the human person, the sense of family, community life, justice, hospitality,

---

10. *Lineamenta*, no. 61.

11. See *Church in Nigeria*, 114.

12. Cf. *Church in Nigeria*, 114; *Nostra Aetatae*, n. 2.

13. *Church in Nigeria*, 115.

14. *Nostra Aetatae*, n. 3.

15. *Ecclesia in Africa*, n. 66.

and solidarity. But *Ecclesia in Africa* also calls for prudent dialogue between Christianity and African Traditional Religion (ATR).[16]

Aware of *Ecclesia in Africa*'s admonition, and writing within the context of the first Synod of the Catholic Diocese of Ikot Ekpene, Vincent Nyoyoko stresses that dialogue with the ATR is necessary even beyond the boundaries and limits of Ikot Ekpene for the following reasons:

- There are many still in our land who practice ATR.

- These adherents are close relations and friends who, in general, are willing to engage in dialogue.

- Many converts from ATR into Christianity retain most of their traditional beliefs. Thus, there is need to formalize the ongoing dialogue in the converts.

- There are many beliefs in ATR that are similar to those in Christianity. The clarification of these through dialogue could enhance their role as basis for "*praeparatio evangelica*," death, morality, and sin.

- The Vatican Council II advocated deeper theological research into each cultural area in order to enable the particular Church to better achieve its identity, and make its contribution to the Universal Church

- Attention to ATR will enhance inculturation and promote evangelization.[17]

By implication, people everywhere, including Nigerians, irrespective of their religion, should pray for peace and work for unity that comes with a change of heart and mentality in various sectors of the society—social, economic, religious, and political.

In Nigeria today, religion has always played a decisive factor in government policy making. That is to say that politics in Nigeria has been mingled with religion to an extent that it has become questionable if Nigeria is still a secular state.

Observing this extreme mingling, Okochi once wrote,

> Our leaders only pay lip service to the concept of secularity while sparing no effort to see that the country is Islamized. This effort has been growing in tenacity and boldness with the passage of time. . . . We have reached a state where all conditions for Islamization

---

16. *Church in Nigeria*, 115; *Ecclesia in Africa*, n. 67.

17. Nyoyoko, "Dialogue and Inculturation," 117–118.

have been fulfilled, save one—the open legal declaration of Nigeria as an Islamic Republic. [18]

Okochi's observation sounds as a warning of the threat to our search for unity and peace. It also implies the total suppression of other religions and its followers. Moreover, suppression is never on the same level with the search for unity. An oppressor, we know, does not get on well with the consciously oppressed. Unity grows out of love, peace, and understanding.

Cases of Islamic assaults, religious violence, and the seeming oppression of Christianity and other religions abound in this country. I have not yet come up with an up-to-date statistic of religious violence, not counting those of the Chibok Schoolgirls' kidnapping. However, in the first edition we noted that between 1980 and 1985, Nigeria experienced five major uprisings sponsored by an Islamic sect known as the *Maitazine*. Below is very old and currently analogically and tabulated statistics of violence, religious oppression, and intolerance, one of the causes of disunity in Nigeria.

Location	Date	Official Death	Arrest
Yahawaki Ward Kono	December 18–20, 1980	4,117	1973
Balunkutu Ward, Maiduguri	October 26, 1982	118	411
Ward, Kaduna	September 26–October 3, 1982	53	116
D. O. Bali Ward, Jimat, Congola	March 27, 1984	68	908
Pantani Ward, Bauchi	April 26–28, 1985	105	295

Between 1985 and 1992 there were a host of other uprisings sponsored by Muslim fanatics and fundamentalists in general. Some of them include: The University of Ibadan crisis of 1985/86; the College of Education, Kafanchan of 1987; the 1991 crisis of Katsina in April, and the May 1991 of Bauchi. We also remember the October 1991 crisis and the August 1993 crisis of Kano. These disturbances resulted in several deaths and the property destroyed worth over one billion naira. [19]

18. Okochi, "Religious Bias," 9.

19. These are the old and 1999 edition's statistics (Udoekpo, 35). No doubt there are

In almost all of these unfortunate crises, the motive was ugly: to suppress, to exterminate. This is why Nigeria prays for a unity yet to be realized in practice and in full.

This is not an attempt to bring down or extol one religion or another. Traditionalists themselves are not better off. They are equally divided. Division among them goes equally to influence the larger sector of the society. These divisions are not only found in Islamic and African Traditional Religions, but also are very acute in the Christian religion. This, along with its responsible factors, affects the functioning of the lager society.

To say that division in Christian religion could also lead and contribute vehemently to an endless search for unity in Nigeria does not reduce our discussion to a mere arithmetic. It calls for identifying the responsible factors and proffering of solutions for a new search and rethinking of the scriptures and the church's teachings.

Nigeria today is becoming a shopping center for all religious groups in the name of Christ. Some of them are:[20]

- Christ Faith Holy Church
- Temple Church
- Brotherhood of the Cross and Star
- Faith Tabernacle Congregation
- Victory Tower Tabernacle
- Qua Iboe Church
- Husterian Church
- Lutheran Church of Nigeria
- Church Faith International
- Church of New Jerusalem
- Holy Ghost Calvary Church
- Christ Evangelical Mission
- True Church of God
- Church of God

---

many new statistics of religious violence in Nigeria and around the world out there beyond the scope of this work.

20. I took these fieldwork statistics as far back as in the 1990s. I want to believe between then and now there have been and increase, though some may have folded.

- Church of Christ
- Christ's Church of God
- Christ Church of Nigeria
- Christ Charity Church
- Methodist Church of Nigeria
- Anglican Church of Nigeria
- Church of Jesus Christ of Latter Day Saints
- The Mission Church
- New Baptist Church
- Christ Followers
- United Christ Power
- Christ Power Apostolic
- The Apostolic Church
- United Apostolic Church
- The Temple Church
- The Mighty Key
- Open Standard Bible Church
- Celestial Church of God
- The Way of Salvation Church of Jesus Christ
- African Church
- African Apostolic Church
- Christ Apostolic Church
- Christ's Baptist Church
- Baptist Church
- Apostolic Faith
- Free Grace Foundation
- Believer's Assembly
- Holy Ghost Apostolic Church
- Holiness of God Mission

- Superlet Church
- Victory Tabernacle
- Wended Baptist Church
- Saint Samuel Spiritual
- Sabbatists
- Divine Love Church
- Adventists
- Presbyterian Church
- Church of the Divine Light
- The Deliverance Tower of Jehovah
- Things to Come Church, etc.
- Assemblies of God
- Jesus Never Fails
- Jesus Overcoming
- Deeper Life
- Salvation Army
- Jehovah Witness
- Christian Deliverance
- The New Baptist Church
- National Church
- Assemblies of Christ
- Victory Chapel
- Greater Evangelism
- Christ for the World Mission
- Sanctified Mount Zion
- Mount Zion Light House
- Full Gospel Church of God
- Mount Zion Full Gospel Mission
- Four Square Gospel Church

- Mount Zion Full Gospel Episcopal

- Christ Ascension Church

- Messiah Church

- Pentecostal Assembly of the World Church

- Royal Family of God Church

- Church of Nazarene

- New Church from Heaven

This list is unending today. Some of them actively assist in our endless search for unity.[21] Many factors may be responsible for this.

WHAT ARE THE RESPONSIBLE FACTORS?

The need to belong is one of the factors responsible for division among Christian communities. The fabric of many communities in Nigeria has been destroyed, and traditional lifestyles disrupted, while many homes are broken up. Some of the above listed groups are organized into small communities in which everyone knows everyone else. They appear to offer a sense of belonging and community, of protection and security. Some of them express and preach prosperity and solidarity to members, a type that sometimes is sustainable.

The search for answers is another factor responsible for division among Christian communities. The modern world offers a bewildering variety of beliefs and values to choose from. Our people feel confused and uncertain. Some of the above listed religious groups, in contrast, appear to offer simple and clear-cut answers to complicated and confusing questions.

Still, many Nigerians feel that the church—for instance, the Catholic Church—has cut them off from traditional religious values. Some of the groups we mentioned recruit successfully because they incorporate styles of worship and preaching close to the cultural traits and aspirations of each Nigerian tribe. The case made by Bishop Robert Barron in his 2019's *Letter to a Suffering Church*, in my opinion, should not be completely swept under the carpet.[22] Many Christians today, both within and outside Nigeria, feel out of touch with themselves, with others, and with their culture and

21. See Fidelis, *Divine Deceit*, 20–24.
22. Barron, *A Suffering Church*.

environment. They feel hurt, abused, and left out. Therefore, new religious groups attract and disharmonize most Nigerian families, although they falsely claim to bring harmony, wholeness, and healing.

Many people in the Catholic Church, for instance, feel they are just another number, a faceless member of a large, impersonal organization. Some of the above listed groups appear to offer the chance to be recognized and to be special. They offer members opportunities to say whatever they feel and to take up leadership. These new groups often offer the strong, charismatic leadership that the seeker failed to find in his family, teachers, or former church leaders. In some of the groups, there is an almost mystical devotion to the spiritual leader, who acts as a powerful building-force in the group and who may be hailed as a "prophet," "guru," or "evangelist."

There is also a sociopolitical need. Many Christians today are fighting for tribal and interstate independence. A Christian from the north feels he should not be led by a Christian leader from the south, and vice-versa.

Others would point to the need for vision as another responsible factor of disunity. People feel worried about violence, conflicts between tribes, conflict within families, the threat of disaster and disease, as well as economic failures. Many of these groups promise members the hope they envision for themselves—hope for their families and businesses.

To sum up, members of these groups seem to live out what they believe with powerful, often magnetic conviction, devotion, and commitment. They go out of their way to meet people where they are, warmly, personally, and directly, making the potential recruit feel very welcome. They also offer participation and assign responsibilities.

They follow up the initial meeting with further contact, with home visits, and offer continuing support and guidance. The new groups help to reinterpret people's experiences, to reassess their values, and they promise answers to life's ultimate questions. They usually provide attractive and convincing literature and audiovisual materials. They often promise healing of the sick and a cure for infertility. They also offer health, happiness, and worldly success. They may present themselves as the only answer, the good news, in a chaotic world.

These are some of the main reasons for the success of these groups, which contribute to disintegration and division in Nigeria and other nations and communities. But the techniques some of them use to recruit and indoctrinate new members are also partly responsible.

Members of the above listed religious groups use highly sophisticated recruitment methods, manipulating potential converts so that they are unable to make a free and fully informed decision. These techniques are:

- Disguising the true identity of the new group of the initial meeting with the potential recruit; the use of a front organization that does not disclose the nature of spirituality that is behind it.

- Overpowering the potential recruit with flattery and affection (love-bombing), offering food and accommodation, money, medicine, and sometimes even sex.

- Demanding unconditional surrender to a guide or leader.

- Isolating the potential recruit from outside information and influence (family, friends, newspapers, radio, and television, etc.), which might break the spell of involvement and the process of absorption into the beliefs and practices of the group.

- Cutting the potential recruit off from his post, concentrating on former mistakes and misdeeds, unsuccessful relationships, and "hang-ups."

- Continually brainwashing the recruits with talks and lectures, slogans, and tricks designed to dull the mind and stop the recruit from thinking for him or herself.

- Keeping the recruit busy and never alone.

- Making sure the recruit is always supervised in order to still doubts and ensure obedience, focusing strongly on the leader.

Consequently, a member of group "A" sees a member of group "B" not only as an arch-Satan, but as an idiot, a fool, and a terrible threat to his means of survival. This same divided spirit is carried into the public sphere—into government offices, schools, the armed forces, the police force, and areas of common sociopolitical and economic interest. Thus, a divided Christianity leads to a divided Nigeria. But Nigeria prays for love, peace, and unity.

It was the original intention of her founder, Jesus Christ, that the Christian Church may be one. This is clearly illustrated in his priestly prayer in John 17:

> I ask not only on behalf of these, but also on behalf of those who
> will believe in me through their word, that they may all be one.
> As you, Father, are in my and I am in you, may they also be in us,

so that he world may believe that you have given me I have given
them, so that they may be one, as we ae one. (John 17:20–21)

This text of unity and its appellation "Jesus' Priestly Prayer" or "High-priestly Prayer" has a long history of development and varied forms of interpretation. It is traceable to the reformation theologian David Chytraeus, who lived from 1531 to 1600. Alttridge, in is article in the *Catholic Biblical Quarterly,* notes that Christians originally called this passage the *praecatio summi sacerdotis.*[23] The Patristic Fathers see in this text the role of Christ expiating sins and interceding for humanity. Rudolf Butlmann prefers to call the text a "farewell prayer of Jesus."[24]

It is an ecumenical text. Commenting pastorally on this passage in his *1992 Lenten Pastoral,* Camillus Etokudoh, then the Bishop of Ikot Ekpene Diocese in Nigeria, noted that Jesus was not only concerned about the unity of his disciples but also prayed for those who would come to faith in him through them. In this prayer, Jesus the high priest stresses unity, faith, love, and peace.[25]

Commenting also on this text, the bishops of the *First Pastoral National Congress of Nigeria,* in discussing ecumenical dialogue, observe that "it cannot be over-emphasized that the realization of Christian unity is a work that transcends human abilities. Therefore, we must place our hope in the prayer of Christ for the Church 'that they may be one' in the love of the Father and the power of the Holy Spirit (cf. John 17:21; Rom 5:5)."[26] This document emphatically points out that divisions among Christians are a scandal to the world, and that Christ wishes his followers to be one with him as he is one with the Father.[27]

Although the history of ecumenism, "to a large extent, parallels the spread of Christianity throughout the ages," it was a priority of the Vatican II.[28] While focusing on promoting Christian unity, Vatican Council II, known as Ecumenical Council, argues that both Catholics and non-Catholics must acknowledge that the fault for the division in Christianity lies

---

23. Attridge, "Priestly Prayer," 11.

24. Bultmann, *Gospel of John,* 486–96.

25. Etokudoh, *"May All Be One,"* 8–9.

26. *Church in Nigeria,* 117.

27. Ibid., 116.

28. See detailed history of ecumenism in Gross, McManus and Riggs, *Ecumenism,* 9–33.

across all Christian denominations.[29] There has to be a U-turn to embrace Christian unity.

This unity must be based on common faith and love, which is the hall-mark of Christianity and the proof to the world that Jesus is the Messiah.

Pope John XXIII, in his encyclical *Aeterna Dei Sapientia,* teaches that the Church must be one because her Bridegroom is one. The Church is that Virgin, the spouse of one Husband, Christ, who allows herself to be corrupted by no error. Thus, throughout the whole world we are to have one entire and pure communion. This remarkable unity of the Church has its wellspring in the birth of God's Incarnate Word. [30] But, unfortunately, the present-day problem in Nigeria witnesses to the fact that Christ's image is now seen from different and diverse egoistic interests. In *The Church in Nigeria* of 1999, the Congress noted that "while there has been significant co-operation within CAN (Christian Association of Nigeria) in apply-ing gospel principles to the sociopolitical and economic dimensions our country, one realizes that the task of greater co-operation in advancing the arts and sciences still leave much to be desired."[31] In other words, there is still work to be done in the area of Christian unity. Theologically, com-petent representatives of Christian churches in Nigeria have yet to "(i) contribute to the mutual understanding of the points of agreement and between the churches; (ii) contribute to the mutual clarification of points of disagreement."[32]

There has to be openness "to goodwill," and dialogue with Christian churches (other churches and denominations) and religious movements, as well as dialogue with members within the Church (episcopal conferences, for instance) and within particular churches (dioceses).[33] Addressing the particular church of Ikot Ekpene Diocese in Nigeria, Nyoyoko again sug-gests that there is an urgent need for an Ecumenical Bible in the vernacular as well as the need to create a CAN chapter in each of our Deaneries.[34]

---

29. See *Unitatis Redintegratio, 7.*

30. *Acterma De Sapentiai.* 12–13.

31. *Church in Nigeria,* 118.

32. Ibid., 118.

33. Ibid., 119–121.

34. Nyoyoko, "Dialogue and Inculturation," 107.

SUMMARY

Beliefs, practices, places, values, leaders, and rituals are essential parts of religion that exist throughout the world, and in Nigeria in particular. The discrimination and disharmony we see in Nigeria can be traced to the disunity we see between the different religions in Nigeria, such as Islam, Christianity, and Traditional Religions. Among the Muslims, there are many different sects and dichotomies, just as there are in Christianity. The disturbing disunity we see in Nigeria's religion spreads into her politics, where power is shared on religious grounds with religious sentiments and passions. This is prevalent in the religious riots we see in schools and universities today.

In the Christian religion, disunity is further demonstrated in the number of churches, groups, and fellowships that occupy our streets and markets today. Perhaps members of these churches want to be healed, to have vision, security, and wealth, to have power, honor, money, absolute freedom, or cultural identity. In the midst of all these, the discussed priestly prayer of Christ in John 17 and various exhortations and teachings of the Church and "good will" of everyone must be our guide in promoting unity in Nigeria and beyond.

3

The Mismanagement of Politics and Unity

THE ABUSE AND MISMANAGEMENT of politics is another major source of disunity. It is not disconnected from the topic of religion, which we discussed in chapter two. Many authors have discussed the mismanagement of politics. But like a Sunday sermon, one must continue to preach both in season and out of season. Like religion, politics is complicated and often a subject of intense debate among friends, colleagues, and even family members.

Politics, from the basic sources of the first edition of *The Limits of a Divided Nation,* is generally and unsophisticatedly documented as a term that has suffered from over-familiarity by different minds and sources. Etymologically, it is derived from two Greek words: *polis* ("city") and *techne* ("art," "skill," "craft," or "method"). Thus, politics would mean the art of organizing men in a society to live and interact with each other to the full realization and actualization of their social nature. It requires the institutionalization of the social structures such as the establishment of legal and governmental systems to facilitate this interaction. The institutions, in turn, organize and consolidate the people for law as a governed, independent, defined sovereign territory—a political society or state; that is a state in its rational and legal nature as an association of moral beings.[1]

1. Nwoko, *Political Theories*, 2.

39

The *Shorter Oxford English Dictionary* states that "Politics is the science and art of government, the science dealing with form, organization and administration of a state or part of one and with the regulations of its relation with other states (imperial, national, domestic, municipal, parochial and foreign)."[2] According to Chris Ejizu, politics is a "dynamic process that entails the mobilization of human and other resources, managing, directing, and enforcing the affairs of public policy and decisions towards the regulation of social order. Put differently, politics applies to different forms of human interest at various levels of society, including the family, village, national, international, church and some purposes in view." [3]

There are still many misconceptions and malpractices of politics that lead to the disintegration of communities and nations. Many people regard politics as a "dirty game" and politicians as "dirty people." That is to say, politics has come to be associated with abuse. This is why Leonardo Boff once said, "For more than a few, politics is something dirty, a lie, a demagoguery,"[4] Some English writers use the term "politics" to refer to the abuse by those who engage in political factions. For instance, Salazar, says Bernard Crick, "detested politics from the bottom of his heart; all those noisy and inherent promises, the impossible demands, the hotchpotch of unfounded ideas and impractical plans . . . all that feverish and sterile fuss."[5]

D'Israeli and Lord Butler similarly offered a negative characterization of politics. As Nwoko explains, "Isaac D'Israeli defines it as the art of governing mankind through deceiving them, and for Lord Butler, it is the art of the possible."[6] Marcel Onyeocha has also observed, "Politics has acquired a rather pejorative sense when referred to any activity of human. Tell someone that he or she is 'bringing politics into this matter,' and he or she will feel as though you have accused him or her of heinous crime."[7]

A large variety of popular views have been offered about politics in different centuries. Plato, Aristotle, St. Augustine, St. Thomas Aquinas, John Locke, Thomas Hobbes, and Nicolo Machiavelli are among those who have devoted time and attention to political life and issues of justice, some of which we discussed in chapter one. Machiavelli, for instance, singled

2. *Shorter Dictionary,* 1062.

3. Ejizu, "Politics," 47–48.

4. Boff, *Church, Charisma and Power,* 11.

5. Crick, *In Defense of Politics,* 15.

6. Nwoko, "Fight for Justice and Right," 4.

7. Onyeocha, *What Is Religious About Religious,* 17–18.

himself out by separating politics and morality. According to him, politics is purely mechanical play of forces without ethical value. What counts for him is the success, irrespective of the means. In other words, the end justifies the means.

On this ground, Jacque Maritain concludes that politics, for Machiavelli, is simply the art of conquering and keeping power by any means. The illusion of Machiavellian politics is immediate success. And this immediate success is for man and not for the state. The state is for the man and not man for the state. To sacrifice man for the success of the state is a misappropriation of the values. The Machiavellian approach to politics, which leads to an unstable nation, is not far from what we see today in Nigerian politics and beyond.

In Nigeria today, due to accumulated ugly experiences, people are saying that politics is a dirty game. Nigerian politicians themselves seem to be saying that it is not only a dirty game, but also a game of money, of majority, and a great instrument of disunity. In fact, corruption, as mentioned in my earlier work in 1994, has become the order of the day, or part of the "abuse of politics" in Nigeria.[8]

Many Nigerian politicians seem to see politics and democracy as synonymous with corruption, crime, and dictatorship. These things do not in any way foster unity. Rather ,they prolong the search for it. Many prominent writers have something to say about the ugly causes for this limitless search for oneness. According to Emmanuel Obunna, "Since Nigeria became independent in 1960, our experiences have been nothing but a vicious circle of democracy followed by corruption."[9]

Adebayo has cautioned that there is a grave feeling that the principal political actors have not learned their lesson from the experience of the First and Second Republics. They are making the same mistakes as before: corruption, hooliganism, loss of lives, and unwillingness to put duty before private gain. The record so far is most discouraging and disquieting. Political aspirants are now boasting about how much they are willing to spend to obtain power, as if public offices and posts are for sale.[10]

Lamenting the abuse of politics, injustice, and corruption, Avisch writes;

8. See Udoekpo, *Corruption in Nigerian Culture* written in 1994, then a student at Bigard Memorial Seminary, Enugu, Nigeria.

9. Obunna, "Root of Violence," 51.

10. Adebayo, "Saving Nigerian Third Republic," 7.

> Those who have power seem now to represent demonic agents of
> death (disunity). These elements of death (disunity) are manifest
> in hunger, disease, poverty, injustices, political apathy, famine,
> Military violence and selfish war . . . They are all problems that
> have their root in political power being in the wrong hands.[11]

The obstacles to the realization of our desired goal—namely, unity in
Nigeria and other places plagued with disunity—include the economic gap
between the rich and the poor, tribalism, ethnicity, and political instability
expressed in tyrannical rule and other forms of immoral behavior.

In Hilary Odili's perspective:

> Why we in the country suffer political instability is because we
> play politics in a manner no mature country ever does. Our own
> politics is a sorry situation. Yes, the country is always a regular
> bedlam of politics. It is sink or swim affair. Survival of the fittest is
> the maxim. Election malpractices and riggings are common, all in
> the name of politics. The people are fooled.[12]

We will return to the issue of corruption in chapter five, drawing
on the biblical case study of Judges 17:1–6. Here, however, we will reflect
briefly on the authentic meaning of politics. Pope John Paul II sees politics
not only as a uniting factor, but also as the "Prudent concern for common
good."[13] Politics, therefore, is not to be understood in negative terms to
mean something other than a tussle between opposing political parties. If
it included this at all, it is only in the positive sense of party competition
to outdo, outpace, or outshine one another in the provision for or effort to
serve the interest of the common good, and not just an interest of the party
in power.[14]

The Christian ethics of politics agrees with Aristotle that politics is not
just good and noble of praise, but it is natural to man. Man is a political ani-
mal. The goal of politics is the common good of all in a given society. This
is why Bernard Haring, an outstanding contemporary Catholic Christian
moral theologian, associates politics with the general welfare or common
interest of all members of society. It is an organized, purposeful activity
for the welfare of society and/or of particular groups in society in view of
the common good. For him, a good political activity is a way of helping to

11. Ibid., 17.

12. Odili, *Sorrows of a Nation*, 53.

13. John Paul II, *Laborem Excercens*, 98.

14. Ngwoke, "Politics," 191.

live faithfully in the freedom and solidarity that befits human dignity and makes possible the attainment of social justice and peace.[15]

Nigeria, in her search, should not hesitate to embrace wholeheartedly this Christian approach as an authentic way forward. This authentic meaning or approach is "opposed to the Machiavellian notion of politics (as earlier discussed) to which politics is a purely mechanical play of force, without ethical values. It stands also in contrast to such views that project politics either as an end in itself or as a means to naked power, prestige and wealth."[16] Therefore, a proper understanding and execution of politics and political power will usher in an end to our endless search for peace and unity in Nigeria. It will also put a limit to corruption.

SUMMARY

In this chapter we have been able to partly establish that abuse and mismanagement of politics and public offices vehemently contributes to our illusive search for unity. Politics is not a dirty game, nor are politicians and military officers dirty people *per se*. Intrinsically, they are supposed to be there for the interest of the people and their various nations. Politics and public service connotes order, protection, defense, love, unity, and peace. Politics is a prudent search for a common good. A realization of the common good brings the realization of the great search for unity and opposes corruption of all kinds, including the type practiced by Micah and his mother, as we'll discuss in chapter five. In the following chapter, we'll discuss abuse of mass media, which is a form of corruption—another factor responsible for disunity.

15. Haring, *Free and Faithful*, 326.
16. Anyanwu, "Politics," 55.

4

Effects of the Abuse of Mass Media
on the Quest for Unity

TODAY NO ONE DOUBTS the fact that media and politics are closely related. Many people, as noted in the first edition of *The Limits of a Divided Nation* in 1999, are increasingly becoming aware of our suppressed need of the sacred in this century, which is characterized by so many remarkable advances in medicine, science, "test tubes," space travel, communication technology, and social media.

These advances in technology raise several questions. In particular, do we really believe in the positive power of communication media in our search for unity? Can Nigerians exist peacefully and harmoniously without the modern phenomena of electronic media? Is mass media necessary for the communal survival of man? Can it contribute in any way to the building up of a nation, which is characterized by the emergence of large groups of people sharing fellowship in social, political, cultural, and religious values?

How does communication media assist in the unity and growth of society? Does it in any way eradicate or mitigate the ills of our society, especially those mentioned in the previous chapters?

Our personal responses mix skepticism and optimism in polyphony in a way that mirrors the double role of mass media in our society. Media has the potential to bring our search for unity to a fruitful end, or to make it a fruitless one. In other words, media can unite us but it can also divide us—depending on how we use the media. Abuse of the media in different parts of the world could be seen as a form of corruption.

By "media" we refer to the means by which information, news, and ideas are disseminated to the people. *The A.U.P. Harrap's Learner's English Dictionary* sees it as "a means of communicating with a large number of people."[1] Vatican Council II's *inter merifica* defines it as "the means of social communication."[2] It as an institution of mass communication—hence, a communication with a mass audience or a large number of people at the same time. This could take various forms, including human speech, print media, video cassette, radio, television, and many others. Its historical development in Nigeria is worth recalling. It may help the present generation to reassess the intention for which media communication systems were founded in Nigeria.

MASS MEDIA DEVELOPMENT IN NIGERIA

Historically, government information services in Nigeria were born out of emergency in the tension that preceded World War II. It was in the wake of World War II that the Colonial Government established an information office in Nigeria as a conduit pipe for information sent from the Ministry of Information, London. Mostly, the information services that suffered a major setback in Nigeria were the electronic media. It was only in 1932 that a broadcasting station was established in Lagos.

Nigeria is a child of circumstances that came to serve certain purposes. Nigeria found herself under colonial rule such that the "native" was totally excluded from the wheel of administration. There was no forum for Nigerian representatives in the government of the people. There was no consultation of the people in decision making. This gave rise to all kinds of resistance. There came the burning need for mass media or means of expression to make government aware of the need for feedback or check and balances. As recorded in my unpublished work *The Place of Mass Media in Nation Building: Nigerian Perspective*, the early press in Nigeria can be categorized under two headings (1) those owned by colonial administrators, and (2) those owned by the early missionaries, although they exist side by side.[3]

1. See *Harrap's Standard Dictionary.*
2. *Inter merifica*, no. 7.
3. Udoekpo, *Mass Media*, 15.

It was in 1859 that a missionary, Rev. Henry Townsend, established the first native language newspaper in Nigeria. The newspaper *Iwe Ironsin Yoruba* was first published in the Yoruba Language at Abeokuta mainly to engender in the Egba people and to build in them the habit of seeking information. The newspaper was a fortnightly production, and it became bilingual in March 1960. It was essentially a religious newspaper for transmitting religious activities to the Egba people. It was not meant for political smearing of opponents or misleading of the public. They laid the foundation for the dissemination of information, but the rate of illiteracy was very high.

Between 1880 and 1937, there were fifty-one newspapers, eleven dailies, thirty-three weeklies, three fortnightlies, and four monthlies. There were also fifteen provincial weeklies in Kano, Calabar, and Port Harcourt. Apart from theses provincial weeklies, all other newspapers were published in Lagos, which remained the most developed newspaper center in Nigeria and Africa.

The early Nigerian newspaper differed from what we have in contemporary Nigeria in two ways. The early Nigerian newspaper did not have the impersonal character of the present power, nor did it have to compete with other vehicles of mass communication. After about five years of monopoly between the government and missionary press, a few individuals, taking advantage of their contacts with the whites, established their own newspapers.

We also notice that the early newspaper expressed a degree of influence that did not relate to the local standard of presentation and modest circulation. The circulation was very poor and the print standard low compared to what we have today. Most of the early practitioners were the reactional journalists, yet they were very popular. The early press was further characterized by poor management and superficial financial bases. And most of the early newspapers eventually folded. Nevertheless, the major reason for their establishment shall not be easily obliterated from our memory.

REASONS FOR EARLY MEDIA DEVELOPMENT IN NIGERIA

The few newspapers in the early 1920s were largely established to create propaganda and political rivalry. Some were intent on making a profit, while others were politically ambitious—there were people whose desire

46

to make money blended with the desire to influence public opinion and advocate consensus for personal and communal ends. And so economic ambitions were often intertwined with philanthropism.

It is interesting to note that from 1914, the Nigerian press assumed a new dimension because the newspaper made some effort to offer a national outlook. All the newspapers began to wear the tag "Nigerian." For instance, *The Nigerian Times*, *The Nigerian Sketch*, and *The Nigerian Chronicle*, which was set up by the Johnson Brothers and existed for only one year because it failed to influence the orientation of its contents.

The Nigerian Times was set up by James Bright Davies, and it seemed to be the most inspiring of the newly emerged Nigerian newspapers. In launching *The Nigerian Times*, Davies declared that he was determined to express opinion and express judgement "freely," frankly, and with open candor. He denounced what he saw as the growing tendency in Lagos newspapers. He pointed out that it was better to promote moral standards than to debase them. To Davies, public opinion was lacking, and it was his desire to "create in Nigeria a strong, healthy and rigorous public opinion." But owing to poor finances, Davies sold *The Nigerian Times* in 1927. By 1928 *The Nigerian Times* was dead.

The Nigerian Pioneer was characterized by continuous abuse of opponents, and it was often accused of secretly serving the interest of the government of Lord Lugard.

The *Nigerian Daily Times*, which was launched on June 1, 1926, set the pace for other newspaper industries in Nigeria. Although it was not the first daily newspaper, by the information of its proprietors, the *Daily Times* encouraged the development of new journalism devoid of attacks on personalities, government, and competitors. It assisted in the creation of journalism intended to inform, educate, and entertain the public.

From the point of view of political development, *Nigerian Daily Times* was not very important when compared to other newspapers. The newspaper was founded as a partnership between certain Nigerians of moderate interest and some European businessmen. Its role as a supporter of colonial government was circumscribed by the demand of commercial realities. By 1936, the publishers of the *Times* decided to fuse with West African Newspapers Ltd. of London and Liverpool. The result of this fusion was a qualitative production, increased revenue base, and an assumed continuity of existence. At that time, some nationalists like Herbert Macaulay and Dr.

Akilade Carlorick saw the activities of the *Nigerian Daily Times* as tending towards anti-nationalism.

In reaction to the *Daily Times,* Herbert Macaulay set up the *Lagos Daily Newspaper,* whose main objective was to launch serious attacks on the *Daily Times.* The newspaper's enemies and political opponents described the *Daily Times News* as the "Penny Lagos Rag," but its admirers referred to it as the "Lagos Penny Paper."[4]

The year 1934 marked yet another professional journal in Nigeria. In 1937, Dr. Nnamdi Azikiwe started the *West African Pilot,* which immediately became the major forum of increased nationalistic consciousness, which had been awaiting an outlet. The *West African Pilot* was an instant success. Zik brought into Nigeria a new idealism of nationalism as well as new techniques of political and journalistic propaganda. So journalism shifted from a violent attack to constructive criticism. Azikiwe demonstrated that one could achieve the same result without attacking the government.

The early newspapers in Nigeria were very weak economically, and this accounted for the short life of most of them. Moreover, *The Nigerian Observer* once remarked: "All along the coast ever since the earliest endeavors were put forth in the direction of the newspaper, this has been the experience of many a heart broken journalist . . . it does not pay."[5] Journalism was by no means a paying venture; rather, it was a thankless task, a risk of time and talent to individual disappointment and popularity.

By 1960 the press had assumed a developed professional standing. The year 1961 saw the direct participation of government in ownership of newspapers, which provided better publicity to its activities. By 1974 all states of the federation, with the exception of Lagos State, established their own newspaper or were associated with joint ownership.[6]

This gives us an insight into the brief historical development of mass media, especially newspapers in Nigeria. Mass media can unite as well as divide us. It is a double-edged sword. It has its tremendous benefits, especially in the modern global village in which we live. Mass media can help in the growth, development, unity, progress, and stability of a nation in a tremendous way. In fact, "every government no matter its ideological

4. See Udoekpo, *Mass Media,* 18–19.
5. *Journalism,* 6.
6. Ibid., 10.

stripes, recognizes some roles for the communication media in national development."[7]

In terms of evangelization, mass media is of vital importance. It helps to disseminate information and contributes greatly to the enlargement and enrichment of people's minds. Put differently, it helps in the propagation of faith and in the consolidation of the kingdom of God. Mass media further promotes the integral development of the person, stimulating dialogue and interpersonal relationships. Mass medial helps to forestall conflict and division as well as enhance commission among peoples, nations, and cultures. Thus, the media promotes human progress.[8]

The advantages of mass media include socialization, education, news offering, economy, and evangelization. Socialization is the process of transmission of culture to the individual. Individuals form not only part of the nation, but they are at the center of the universe. The individual gives meaning and sufficient interpretation to the structures formed in our society, including structures that promote unity.

Socialization begins early in life and continues in death. Mass media has proved important for effective and adequate socialization that leads to a solid and well-built Nigeria. It educates and informs citizens of what society expects of them through different types of suitable programs as well as morally justifiable broadcasts, write-ups, and motion pictures.

In terms of education, mass media supplements and compliments the existing facilities for the self-fulfillment and development of individual potential, which in the long run facilitates the development and building of Nigeria as a united entity. This is why Ekwelie writes that;

> The Mass Media of mass communication has a significant assignment in spreading general information as well as formal education. Britain now has the University of the Air in which citizens depend for their formal education. The Chinese have been using a similar system to spread education to distant places in other vast countries . . . . In the case of Nigeria, the attempt to teach by radio has spanned the whole period of hunger for mass education.[9]

Additionally, in a 1951 report, a British official, then working for the Nigerian broadcasting services as a producer of radio Nigeria, described radio as the most powerful medium for influencing and educating people.

7. Ekwelie, "Mass Media," 206.

8. Illoghalu, "Communication Media," 36.

9. Ekwelie, "Mass Media," 212.

He further described it as the "most potent mass disseminator of culture and information."[10] Thus, through radio, television, newspapers, magazines, journals, pamphlets, and social media sites like Facebook and Twitter, whether secular or ecclesiastical, Nigerian children have the advantage of learning quickly about the need for health care, natural family planning, respect for life and the sacred, and human dignity as well as the need to defend their legal and constitutional rights.

In addition to socialization and education, mass media helps nations to develop through its function of news offerings. By "news" we mean, in the words of Willard Bleyer, "anything timely that interests a large number of persons."[11] Mass media offers news items on a regular basis. One objective of the news is:

> An attempt to help develop an informal citizenry. The idea is to bring more and more Nigerians into a participant-political culture. So when newspapers and magazines devote their columns to what the leaders are doing and saying, the idea is that readers should follow the activities of their leaders so as to equip, to pass informal judgment [upon the] masses and thereby kill lethargy among them.[12]

Mass media also affects the economy in Nigeria, as well as the economies of other nations.

As mentioned earlier, mass media plays a role in evangelization. By "evangelization" here we mean to announce Christ, to proclaim Christ, and to communicate Christ and his gospel to the world. Evangelization means, "bringing the Good News into all the strata of humanity, and through its influence transforming humanity from within, and making it new."[13] Evangelization requires effort from the church both to plant the faith and to consolidate it. But to accomplish *unum necessarium* fully, the church must properly employ modern means of social communication because mass media reaches an unlimited audience. Using various forms of media, pastors can reach and influence far more people in our secular society for the growth and development of Nigeria. This is why it is stressed in the Code

---

10. See *Nigerian Broadcasting*, 8–9.

11. *Introduction to Journalism*, 19.

12. Ekwelie, "*Mass Media*," 209.

13. Pope Paul VI, *Evangelii Nuntiandi*, no. 18, as expanded on in chapter 6.

that "in exercising their office the pastors of the church are to make ample use of the means of social communication."[14]

In sum, the importance of mass media for the unity and progress of a given nation cannot be overemphasized, particularly if their code of conduct is kept and not neglected or abused. In Nigeria, the code of conduct for journalists stipulates that:

a. It is the moral duty of a journalist to have respect for the truth and publish only the truth.

b. The public is entitled to truth and the correct and accurate information that can form the basis for sound journalism as well as ensure the confidence of the people.

c. It is the duty of every journalist to publish only facts and never to suppress or slant facts for selfish ends.

d. It is the duty of every journalist to refuse gratification for the publication or suppression of news or comments.

e. The journalist shall employ all legitimate means in the collection of news and shall defend always the right to free access to news, provided due regard is paid to privacy.

Having seen what the code of conduct for Nigerian journalists has to say, the following questions could be raised for further reflection:

- To what extent have media men and women been respecting the rights of Nigerian citizens?

- How many would foster unity through their confidence and trust in Nigerian journalists?

- How many media men and women today would, like the late Dele Giwa, the founding editor of *Newswatch Magazine,* refuse gratification, and political appointment for a publication or suppression of news and truth?

In light of these questions, Aghaulor observes that "media practitioners of our day are more interested in reporting and publishing misdemeanors of this society in order to make news. We often hear of nations engaged in war. But, how often do we hear of those at peace being commended."[15]

14. *Code of Canon Law,* c. 822.
15. Aghaulor, "Power of Communication," 37–38.

In other words, our media men and women sometimes delight in inciting a section of the country against another section, or stirring controversies or reporting falsely just to make news or economic gain. This often leads to disunity. There has to be a limit to unfounded reporting and abuse of the media. As noted by Okere, "It is the special duty of the news radio to create a justice-oriented attitude in society. Journalists should create societies conscience by jealously defending their right and courageously are apportioning."[16] Yet the reverse seems to be the case in today's society. We see various misuse of media, including pornographic displays, abuse of the political process, and the search for material gain and wealth.

Politicians often use mass media to exploit, deceive, and fool the poor masses. They give people the false impression that politics is a dirty game—a game characterized by corruption, lies, deception, injustice, tribalism, discrimination, and disunity. Today, because of media misinformation, great percentages of citizens are influenced and have this false impression that politics is characterized by deception, wanton and empty polemics, circumvention of the law, exploitative social maneuvering, aggressive partisanship, and discrimination."[17]

Arguably, such misinformation is also motivated by the inordinate search for material gain without a parallel spiritual and moral advancement. Some people trade news and information for personal gain and self-gratification, without taking cognizance of the unity of the nation.

Does our existing government caution our media men and women to be conscious of their duty for the interest and unity of the nation? Why are most pages of our dailies used for advertising goods, title receivers, tribal political groups, and other private interests when they could be used for moral essays that would benefit all people? The effects of the abuse of mass media on contemporary society cannot be overemphasized.

SUMMARY

For some of us, this may be a difficult chapter to read. Whatever you are able to get out of this chapter, keep in mind that mass media has the potential to contribute to the growth, progress, development, and stability of our nation. It serves as an effective disseminator of information, news, and opinion. It is also a good agent of socialization. It has advantageous in the

16. Okere, "Lift Up Your Heart."
17. Nwoko, " An Address," 3–4.

areas of education, economy, political life, recreation, inspiration, and in evangelization of the people God.

On the other hand, the negative effects of media can be devastating, particularly when the media is devoted to pornography, false news, and misinformation or exists for profit with no concern for ethics.

In using media, we much consider the culture, morality, and customs of our age. It is also the duty of the media to protect and raise to a good standard the culture of our people. Economically, it would be unfair to exploit the underdeveloped aspects of the Nigerian or African cultures, customs, and beliefs for better personal material wealth. True notions of politics and political orientations must be inculcated in our people through the mass media. This will in turn promote a fruitful search for unity. The media should remain the custodians of truth, peace, unity, harmony, togetherness, communal spirit, justice, and true democracy. Media must not be corrupt and divisive.

5

Lessons from Micah's Corruption
in Judges 17:1–6

CORRUPTION IS ANOTHER SAD phenomenon that divides our world today. This chapter engages in a biblical discussion of the ugly phenomenon of corruption as a source of disunity by examining the book of Judges.[1] The book of Judges, which tells of a period characterized by corruption, idolatry, moral depravity, violence, deception, disobedience, war, rape, murder, kidnapping, spiritual confusion, lack of leadership, political fragmentation, and unethical relativism, can serve as a lesson for us today.

In Judges 17:1–6 we find an Ephraimite named Micah who confesses to stealing eleven hundred pieces of silver from his mother. After Micah returns the silver, his mother refashions two hundred pieces of it into a carved and molten idol (*pesel ûmassēkāh*) for YHWH worship (Judg 17:3–4; cf. 18:24, 27) and keeps the remaining nine hundred pieces. Rather than reproof Micah for this theft, she rejoices over the silver and blesses her corrupt and covetous child.

Both Micah and his mother seem to portray a lack of knowledge and fear of the Lord (Judg 17:7–13). Their spiritual confusion, greed, fear, covenantal breakdown, and moral misbehavior resounds throughout Judges 17–21. Their corrupt behavior is not only palpable but breaks the

---

1. Some of the materials used in this chapter were shared at the 12th CABAN Convention on "Integrity and Corruption in the Bible" on November 5–8, 2019, in Akure, Nigeria.

Ten Commandments (Exod 20:1–17; Deut 5:6–21). The account in Judges 17 invites us as Nigerians and members of the church and religious communities to not only look back to the morality teachers in Judges and in the Deuteronomistic tradition as a whole, but also to respond to the Lord's covenant and reassess our communities and nations, which are currently plagued with similar forms of corruption.

In this chapter, we will contextually and theologically reexamine Judges 17:1–6 in the Nigerian context, where there is sustained discontent about corruption. In Nigeria we find testimonies of corruption and discontent written in the pages of daily newspapers, written works, books, literature reports, journals, and magazine commentaries.[2] A brief reappraisal of some of these testimonies will benefit this chapter in several ways:

1. It situates the problem culturally and sheds light on why there has been some global ambivalent feelings about Nigeria and her integrity.

2. It offers us wider perspectives for understanding the meaning, types, histories, and nature of corruption in Nigeria.

3. It prepares for the comparison of the Nigerian situation with the narrative texts of Judges, which follows.

4. It anticipates our conclusion that in spite of humanity's corrupt nature, God is mercifully at work in recreating us in hope, trust, love, obedience, and faithfulness.

LITERATURE ON CORRUPTION IN NIGERIA (LCN)

Much of the literature on corruption in Nigeria (LCN) sees corruption from bipartite perspectives: physically and morally. Physically, there is "destruction of anything, especially, by disintegration or by decomposition . . . dissolution or destruction of what constitutes the essence of a thing."[3] Morally, corruption "is the perversion or destruction of integrity in the discharge of public duties . . . bribery or favoritism."[4] Corruption "is the perversion

---

2. Some of the literature on corruption in Nigeria include; Udoekpo, *Corruption in Nigerian Culture*; Smith, *A Culture of Corruption*; Oji and Oji, *Corruption in Nigeria*; Briggs, *How to Fight Corruption*; Faleye, "Religious Corruption"; Itebiye, "Corruption in Nigerian"; Okonjo-Iweala, *Fighting Corruption;* Uwaifo So, "Corruption."

3. Udoekpo, *Corruption in Nigerian Culture*, 11.

4. Udoekpo, *Corruption in Nigerian Culture*, 12.

of integrity or state of affairs through bribery, favour or moral depravity."[5] Culturally, phrases such as "impairment of virtue," "lack of integrity or honesty," and "deceit and violation of established rules" have also been used to describe the situation in Nigeria.[6] Oji calls it ethical decay, indiscipline, and a social malady that dates back to the colonial era (1914).[7]

Daniel Jordan Smith, an American anthropologist, and Ngozi Okonjo-Iweala, one-time Nigerian minister for finance and managing director of World Bank, both have written significant LCN that situates and compares Nigeria's situation with that narrated in the book of Judges. In describing the awareness of corruption in Nigeria, Smith and Okonjo-Iweala capture the popular ambivalent feelings about Nigeria. They notice, on the one hand, that Nigerians are known to be outgoing, warm, ambitious, confident, vibrant, and entrepreneurial, especially Nigerian women.[8] On the other hand, "Nigeria can be a very difficult place."[9] Like in the case of Micah and his mother in Judges 17 (soon to be examined), Okonjo-Iweala in particular notices that "the actions of a small percentage of Nigeria's population have given the country a bad name; one associated with corruption."[10] It is becoming a way of life, a culture in Nigeria. Everybody talks loudly, preaches and debates about it, yet nothing substantially has been done to mitigate corruption.

Smith notes that "when Nigerians talk about corruption, they refer not only to stories or the abuse of state offices for some kind of private gain but also to a whole range of social behaviors in which various forms of morally questionable deception enable the achievement of wealth, power, or prestige as well as much more mundane ambition."[11] Some of these mundane ambitions are uniquely found at police checkpoints, where motorists offer banknotes in exchange for safe passage. They are also found at the internet cafés, where thousands of young Nigerians craft their notorious e-mail scam letters.[12] Corruption is additionally found at "local nongovernmental organizations (NGOs) created to siphon international donor dollars into

5. See the *Oxford English Dictionary*.
6. Briggs, *How to Fight Corruption*, 1–8.
7. Oji and Valerie U. Oji, *Corruption in Nigeria*, 1–3.
8. Okonjo-Iweala, *Fighting Corruption*, xv.
9. Smith, *Corruption*, xi.
10. Okonjo-Iweala, *Fighting Corruption*, xv.
11. Smith, *Corruption*, 5.
12. See Smith (*Corruption*, 28–52) for classic examples of such e-mail scams.

individual hands."[13] Culturally, Nigerian notions of corruption "encompass everything from government bribery and graft [what Nigerians call fraud, taken from a section in the Nigerian criminal code that describes these crimes], rigged election and fraudulent business deals, to the diabolical abuse of occult powers, kidnapping, medical quackery, cheating in school, and even deceiving a lover."[14]

These corrupt practices in Nigeria can be categorized within the seven typological forms identified in Giorgio Blundo and Jean-Pierre Olivier de Sardan's comparative study of corruption in three other West African countries (Benin, Niger, and Senegal).[15] These seven forms are:

1. commission for illicit services (e.g., a contractor might provide money to a government official to ensure that he or she receives a job in a process supposedly based on competitive bids, or an importer might pay a customs official to underestimate the value of their good to reduce a tariff)

2. unwarranted payment for public services (e.g., paying extra money for basic services, usually provided free, like issuance of licenses, passports, and birth certificates)

3. gratuities (e.g., providing "dash" or "bribe," for services, even when poorly done)

4. string pulling (e.g., using social and political influence to promote favoritism, offering preferential access to employment, education etc., based on who you know)

5. levies and tolls (e.g., police who collect tolls from motor vehicle drivers at roadside checkpoints, or bureaucrats who require pensioners to pay money in order to receive their pensions)

6. sidelining (using company or official resources for private purposes such as using official vehicles for personal travel, running a private clinic in a public facility, or using university resources to conduct a private consulting job)

13. Smith, *Corruption*, 5.

14. Smith, *Corruption*, 5.

15. See Giorgio Blundo and Jean-Pierre Olivier de Sarden ("La corruption," 106–118) for details of these various classifications.

7. misappropriation (e.g., public materials are not just used for private purposes but expropriated entirely)[16]

Lengthy stories about and practical examples of these forms of corruption that have brought untold hardship and shame to many Nigerians abound in cited LCN. However, they are beyond the scope of this chapter.[17]

This is not to say that Nigerians hold the monopoly on corruption. No, corruption is not limited to Nigeria. Like greed, it is a global nightmare.[18] It comes in different shapes and forms in different continents, countries, cultures, and times. From biblical times, pre-dating Nigeria, we find stories of corruption, idolatry, moral depravity, violence, deception, disobedience, war, rape, murder, kidnapping, spiritual confusion, sociopolitical, moral fragmentation, and unethical relativism. All this can be found in the morality tale of Micah in Judges 17–21, and in the broader context of the Deuteronomistic tradition.

THE SITUATION IN JUDGES

Modern scholarship treats the book of Judges as an important historical source for the time period between the exodus from Egypt and the beginning of the united monarchy.[19] The 21 chapters of Judges contain stories of God's faithfulness and the Israelites' (including Israelite judges, kings, and ordinary people) unfaithfulness.[20] They are stories of sin and punishment, repentance, restoration, and salvation. Although these stories have been discussed in the past in different historical settings, reexamining them in

16. See also Smith (*Corruption,* 17–18) for further details on these seven forms of corruption.

17. These stories revolve around scam e-mail letters, over invoiced contracts, dead expatriates' bank accounts, a deceased dictator's desperate widow, 419, diabolical rituals like the "otokoto hotel Owerri saga" (1996), etc.

18. Some of the following works have also captured the global nature of corruption: Réne ("Globalization of Greed," 43–67); Arroyo ("Corruption," 83–102); Bullón, ("Notes on Corruption," 11–28); Alvarado ("Facing Corruption Today," 29–44); Onyumbe ("Interrupting Our Journeys," 263–270).

19. Schneider, *Judges,* xii.

20. It is evident, e.g., in McKenzie (*Introduction to the Historical Books,* 57–58); Branick (*Understanding Historical Books,* 31), that based on content, many scholars usually attribute three major parts to the 21 chapters of Judges: (a) introduction (Judg :1–3:6); (b) stories about individual Judges (Judg 3:7–16:31); and (c) the concluding stories (Judg 17–18).

this chapters brings to mind the unique experiences in Nigeria and those of our brothers and sisters all over the world who have been wounded by violence, corruption, and poor leadership.[21] They are cyclical stories lamenting the idolatry and corruption practiced by families, religious leaders, and political leaders when there was "no king in Israel; all the people did what was good in their own eyes" (Judg 2:10–19, 17:6; 18:1; 19:1; 21:25).

Judges 17–21 provides the broader context for Judges 17:1–6. Following the accounts of the individual judges in Judges 1–16, this section tells stories about Micah and his mother, the Levites, and the migration of the Danites. Olson rightly observes that these stories portray the systematic corruption and breakdown of nearly all of the Ten Commandments (Exod 20:1–17; Deut 5:6–21). Israelites worship other gods and idols (Judg 17:3–5), take the name of the Lord in vain (Judg 17:13), dishonor their parents (Judg 17:1–2), brutally kill innocent victims (Judg 18:27; 19:26–29; 21:10), commit adultery and rape (Judg 19:22–25), steal property (Judg 17:2; 18:21–27), bear false witness (Judg 20:1–7), and covet what belongs to their neighbors (Judg 18:27–31; 21:8–24).[22]

Affirming Olson, Mueller calls Micah's stories a "morality tale framed by an author who stands in the Deuteronomic tradition . . . the protagonists are mired in fear, idolatry and immorality."[23] Like stories we hear on Nigerian media, literature (LCN), and daily conversation, the characters in Micah's tales covet, dishonor their parents, take the Lord's name in vain, lie, steal, kill, kidnap, and make carved images (*pesel ûmassēkāh*), *ephod*, and *teraphim* (*ʾēphôd ûtərāphîm*), and place them in shrines dedicated to the Lord.[24]

ENTERING THE TEXT FOR CONTEMPORARY SOCIETY

Mueller is quick to point out that the markings and divisions in the Hebrew text (*MT*) indicate that there are about eight subdivisions to Micah's morality story:

21. See Mueller (*Morality Tale,* 1–49) for an impressive historical survey of scholarly contributions on the Micah story (Judg 17–18).

22. Olson, "Judges," 864–65.

23. Mueller, *Morality Tale,* 51–52.

24. Mueller, *Morality Tale,* 52.

1. Judges 17:1–6

2. Judges 17:7–13

3. Judges 18:1–6

4. Judges 18:7–10

5. Judges 18:11–14

6. Judges 18:15–20

7. Judges 18:23–26

8. Judges 18:27–31[25]

These eight subdivisions can be grouped under three major topics, blocks, or themes:

1. Micah and his mother (Judg 17:1–6)

2. Micah and the Levite (Judg 17:7–13)

3. the Danites' migration and establishment of sanctuary at Dan (Judg 18:1–31)[26]

Our discussion will be focusing on the story of Micah and his mother in Judges 17:1–6, which says in the *NRSV*:

> 1 There was a man in the hill country of Ephraim whose name was Micah. 2 He said to his mother, "there eleven hundred pieces of silver that were taken from you, about which you uttered a curse, and even spoke it in my hearing,—that silver is in my possession; I took it; but now I will return it to you." And his mother said, "May my son be blessed by the LORD!" 3 Then he returned the eleven hundred pieces of silver to his mother; and his mother said, "I consecrate the silver to the LORD from my hand for my son, to make an idol of cast metal." 4 So when he returned the money to his mother, his mother took two hundred of silver, and gave it to the silversmith, who made it into an idol of cast metal; and it was in the house of Micah. 5 This man Micah had a shrine, and he made an ephod and teraphim, and installed one of his sons, who

---

25. I am referring to such markings as the *sôph pasûq* (:) and the *pethûḥā* (פ), accessible in Scott (*A Simplified Guide*, 1).

26. For classification of these subdivisions and three major themes or blocks, see Noth ("Background of Judges 17–18," 69–71); Amit ("Hidden Polemic," 7); Webb (*Judges*, 182–188); Becker (*Richterzeit und Königtim*, 227–228).

became his priest. 6 In those days there was no king in Israel; all the people did what was right in their own eyes.

This passage introduces the character as *Mîkāyhû* (Judg 17:1, 4), a name that literally means "who is like YHWH," and Michael, "who is like God" ("*anietie nte Abasi*" in Efik). This name expresses the notion of God's incomparability.[27] Eight other people answer to this name in the Hebrew Bible.[28] Oslon argues that *Mîkāyhû* "implies that no god, idol, or other representation can ever compare with or substitute for the Lord."[29] That is to say that the Lord resists being corrupt, bought over, bribed, fooled, or being captured or led astray by any corrupt individual or institution of any nation.

In verse 5 and in the rest of the story, the shorter form Micah (*Mîkâ*) is attested. Some scholars argue that Micah is an abbreviated form of *Mîkāyhû* or a product of a textual problem.[30] Zevith thinks the variation reflects two sources.[31] Another interpretation widely held by scholars is that the writer is being ironic about Micah's corrupt behavior when there was no good leadership in Israel (Judg 17:6; cf. 18:1; 19:1; 21:25). Since this passage serves as a polemic against the northern worship, it is most likely that the narrator chose the shortened form of Micah for ironic, divine-distancing purposes, "the person whose name glorifies God, by suggesting his incomparability, as a thief who helped establish illegitimate worship."[32]

Micah returns to his mother eleven hundred pieces of silver that he had stolen; this is a fat sum, equal to what Delilah received for betraying her lover Samson (Judg 16:4). Micah's mother fashioned two hundred of the silver pieces into a molten image (Judg 17:1–5). This delighted her son Micah, who installed his own son to serve at the shrine where this false

27. Boling, *Judges*, 255.

28. These additional eight people listed by Brettler ("Micah [Person]," 806–7) include, (1) great grandson of Saul (2 Sam 9:12), (2) Son of Imlah, an Israelite during the time of Ahab and Jehoshaphat (1 Kgs 22), (3) the father of one of the members of the delegation sent by King Josiah to Huldah (2 Kgs 22:12), (4) a prophet in the book of Micah, (5) a descendant of Reuben (1 Chr 5:5), (6) a Levite in Jerusalem (1 Chr 9:15; Neh 11:17), (7) a Levite, eldest son of Uziel (1 Chr 23:30), (8) one of the signatories in Neh 10:12. In the *LXX* he is *Micha, Michas* in the Vulgate, and Micah in Efik Bible, *Edisana Nwed Abasi*.

29. Olson, "Judges," 869.

30. See this position in Mueller, *Morality Tale*, 55.

31. See Labushchagne, *Incomparability of Yahweh*; Zevith, "Israelite Personal Names," 12.

32. Brettler, "Micah," 806; Mueller, *Morality Tale*, 53.

god was kept. Micah later replaced his son with an itinerant Levite (Judg 17:7–13), a descendant of Moses (Judg 18:30), whom the Danites later kidnapped along with the cult statues (Judg 18).[33] Like the actions of some corrupt Nigerians, which have given Nigeria a reputation for corruption, Micah's immoral actions reflect the actions of the Israelites when there was no responsible leadership (Judg 17:6; 18:1; 19:1; 21:25).[34]

In Judges 17:2 Micah confesses to the theft under oath and threat of curse (*'ālâ*) to his mother, whose name is unknown.[35] She is referred to as `*immô* ("his mother," *mētēr autou*" in the *LXX*, "*eka esie*" in Efik, and *matri suae* in Latin) about six times (2x in v. 2; 3x in v. 3, and 4x in v. 4). It is puzzling that Micah's mother is not named given her significant role in this morality tale. Yee suggests that Micah's mother is Delilah, who betrayed Samson for eleven hundred pieces of silver in Judges 16:5, 18.[36]

Upon hearing Micah's confession, his mother (*eka esie, matri suae*) blesses him rather than reproofs. It seems to me that when Micah began to confess, he was afraid to directly own up to his mistake. He indirectly and passively says to his mother, "the eleven hundred pieces of silver which were taken from you," (`*eleph ûmē'āh hakkeseph `āšer luqqaḥ-lāk*), using the verb *lāqaḥ* ("to take") in the passive *luqqaḥ-lāk* ("taken from you," *ekebode fi*). Like most morally corrupt people, it took Micah a while to say, "behold, the silver is with me, I took it" (*hinnēh- hakkeseph `ittî `ănî ləqaḥttiw*).

The details given in these verses speak to the depraved moral character of Micah and his mother. In Oslon's view, "one senses the total absence of accountability and responsibility in this family."[37] It also reminds us of instances in Nigeria and beyond, where family members celebrate their sons and daughters who return home from public office with looted and stolen wealth. Ironically, these looters, like Micah's mother, sometimes describe their bad behaviors as "blessings from God."

As if the initial verses were not ironic enough, in Judges 17:3 Micah's mother consecrates the stolen eleven hundred pieces of silver to the Lord on behalf of her son "to make a carved and molten image"(*la'ăsôth pesel ûmassēkāh*). Micah then returns it back to the mother (*wə'attāh `ăšîbhennû lāk*).

---

33. Brettler, "Micah," 806.

34. Olson, "Judges," 869.

35. We have seen this before in Judges 11 (Jephthah's daughter), Judges 13 (Samson's mother), and in Judges 19 (the case of the Levite's concubine).

36. Yee, "Ideological Criticism," 158.

37. Olson, "Judges," 870.

Yet in Judges 17:4 Micah's mother gives the silversmith only two hundred pieces of silver to make into idols of "cast metal" (*pesel ûmassēkāh*) for her son's house (*bəbêth mîkāyhû*). The text notes that Micah had a shrine (*bêth 'ĕlōhîm*), literally a "house of God/gods," with an ephod and teraphim; he enlisted his son to minister at his private shrine (Judg 17:5).

In an attempt to better explain this passage, source and textual critics have noticed some textual difficulties in Judges 17:2–5. For instance, Wellhausen and Becker consider Judges 17:2–4 to be a later addition (gloss).[38] Others assign these verses to different sources (vv.1 and 5 to J and vv.2–4 to E).[39] Auld believes that vv.1–4 are "a fragment of an earlier story on which the present one has been built."[40] In spite of this textual debate, most commentators believe that an error took place during the copying and transmitting of the manuscript text. Scholars suggest the statements "and now I will return it to you" (*wə'attāh 'ăšîbhennû lāk* = Efik "*modo ndiyak enee no fi ndien*") at the end of v. 3, and "and then he returned the silver to his mother" (*wayyāšebh 'et-hakkeseph lə 'immô* = Efik "*ntre ke enye ayak silver oro ono eka esie*") in the beginning of v. 4 in the *MT* were omitted from the end of v. 2, where they originally belong.[41] Boling in particular suspects the "displacement was triggered by confusion of 'archaic' and 'modern' uses of prepositions."[42] This confusion or misplacement of words and statements could also have been a result of the turmoil that went on in the minds of Micah and his mother. Similarly, instances abound in the *LCN* where those caught in corruption in Nigeria and elsewhere offer conflicting statements about their inordinate wealth.

Besides some of these textual errors and problems, certain words are used repeatedly in the text to convey significant theological points. For instance, the author uses the verb *šûbh* ("to return," "to restore") twice (vv. 3–4, *wayyašebh*) to convey that Micah returned the stolen money to his mother. Micha says, "I now return it back [or hand it over] to you" using the *hiphil*, first person common singular (3rd person masculine singular suffix) with "energetic nun" (*wə'attāh 'ăšîbhennû lāk/kai apodōsō soi auto*).

---

38. Wellhausen (*Die Composition*, 232) and Becker (*Richterzeit und Königtum*, 230, 253) views verses 2b–3abc as secondary.

39. See Moore, *Judges*, 367–368; Burney, *Book of Judges*, 409–417; Mueller, *Morality Tale*, 54.

40. Auld, *Joshua, Judges, and Ruth*, 224.

41. See opinions of scholars who engage in this textual debate in Täubler, *Biblische Studien*, 46; Polzin, *Moses and the Deuteronomist*, 195, and Boling, *Judges*, 256.

42. Boling, *Judges*, 256

Other verbs with great theological or didactic significance include *lāqaḥ* ("to take") and `āsâ ("to make"). The use of these three verbs (*šûbh, lāqaḥ* and `āsâ*) suggests not only taking/stealing and returning for the purpose of "making" cultic devices (carved and molten images), but can also mean change of loyalty, restoration, and repentance to turn back from evil to God or from good to evil.[43]

It is also worth noting that throughout this story, Micah's mother's actions set "Micah's household on the course of idolatry and in time, an entire tribe follows in her footsteps."[44] Instead of turning back to God after breaking the Ten Commandments (coveting, stealing, dishonoring parents, being slow to own up to mistakes, and taking the Lord's name in vain, Judg 17:2), as is typical of corrupt officials (especially in Nigeria), Micah and his mother repeatedly tossed the silver to each other (Judg 17:2–4). Finally, Micah turned to idolatry and made an ephod—imitating priestly garments used in worship of the true God. Micah also made a teraphim, a household idol for worship connected to hope of prosperity and protection. Micah also installed one of his sons as his priest in his private shrine, known as *bêth* `ĕlōhîm, that is, "house of God/gods" (Judg 17:5).[45]

Commenting on this house of gods, Mueller points out that Micah's house is the only shrine (*bêth* `ĕlōhîm) in the *MT* where carved and molten images (*pesel ûmassēkāh*) are assembled together with ephod and teraphim (Judg 17:5; 18:14, 17, 18).[46] Upon second look, *bêth* `ĕlōhîm may mean "a house of God," "a house of gods," or "hand-made gods," since the author seems to deliberately omit the definite article. By doing this, the author draws a contrast between Micah's house of God (*bêth* `ĕlōhîm) and the house of God (*bêth hā* `ĕlōhîm, Judg 18:31) at Shiloh (1 Sam 1:7, 24; 3:15).[47]

Scholars insist that the ephod and teraphim (*ephoud kai theraphin, LXX*) installed in Micah's house shrines are closely associated with items

---

43. For an extensive study of *šûbh* see Preuschen ("Die Bedeutung von שבות שוב im Alten Testament," 1–74); Dietrich (שבות שוב, *Die Endzeitliche Wiederherstellung bei den Propheten*); Baumann ("שבות שוב , eine exegestische Untersunchung," 17–44); Borger ("16–315 ",שבות שוב); Holladay (*Root Šûbh in the Old Testament*); Bracke ("*šûb šebût*: A Reappraisal," 233–244); and Soggin ("שוב , Šûb, to return," 1312–1317).

44. Cf. Mueller, *Morality Tale*, 54.

45. *pesel ûmassēkāh (MT)= Oikos Theou* in *LXX* and *ufok Abasi* in Efik Bible.

46. *Glupton kai chōneuton* in *LXX* and *edisoi mbiet ye editara mbiet* in Efik Bible.

47. Mueller, *Morality Tale*, 60. We have *bêth yehovah/ădōnay* ("the [house of YHWH]") in 1 Sam 1:7; 24; 3:15.

for divination (1 Sam 23:9).[48] The ephod is widely known to be a priestly vestment that is elaborately made.[49] However, it can also refer to "a robe of approach to God; items representing deity, used in consulting deity."[50] Alternatively, an ephod could be a box that functions as a tool for the casting of lots before the Lord.[51] *Tərāphîm* are probably a type of anthropomorphic household god used for divination (Gen 31:19, 34–35; 1 Sam 19:13, 16; 2 Kgs 23:24; Zech 10:2; Ezek 21:21).[52]

Micah and his mother's idolatry, stealing, coveting, lies, hesitation to repent and return stolen goods, and lack of fear of the Lord imply that corruption has become the order of the day in Israel. Religion had become twisted and distorted, as it has in some worship places in Nigeria today. Olson puts this well when he observes that in Micah's day, "curses become blessings. Consecration to the Lord becomes idolatry. Vows of offering are only partially fulfilled."[53] All this mirrors the corruption and increasing estrangement of Micah and his generation from the Lord (Judg 17:1–5, 12; 18:14, 17, 18) and reminds us Nigerians that similar stories abound in our communities and constituencies, some of which have been entrusted to our leaders (civil, ecclesiastical, and traditional).

LEADERSHIP AND CORRUPTION

Verse 6 sums up Micah's morality tale (Judg 17:1–5) with the refrain "in those days there was no king in Israel, and everyone did what was right in their own eyes" (*bayyāmîm hāhēm ʾên melek bəyiśrāʾēl, ʾîš hayyāšrār bəʿênâw yaʾăseh*). Many have rightly observed that this comment reflects the religious and moral chaos *vis-à-vis* poor leadership, authentic kingship, and relativism in ancient Israel, as exemplified in the story of Micah's household shrine in Judges 17. This refrain-formula functions as an overarching commentary on the entire period described in Judges 17–21.

---

48. Hamlin, *At Risk in the Promised Land,* 147.

49. Klein, *The Triumph of Irony,* 150; Van der Toorn and Lewis, "תרפים tərāphîm, אפוד ʾephodh, בד badh," 772; and Boling, *Judges,* 256.

50. See Soggin, *Joshua,* 265; Gray, "Idolatry," 677.

51. Budde, "Ephod und Lade," 12–13.

52. Cf. Mueller, *Morality Tale,* 60.

53. Olson, "Judges," 870.

This formula is repeated in Judges 18:1; 19:1; and 21:25, and thus brackets the entire concluding section of the entire book of Judges. [54]

Wilson concludes that "the formula at 17:6 prepares us for the short-hand version at 18:1 and 19:1: 'In those days Israel had no king.' "[55] He argues that this is similar to the technique used in Judges 1–16 (cf. Judg 2:11; 3:7, 12; 4:1; 6:1; 10:6; 13:1), where the phrase "The Israelites did what was evil in the sight of the Lord" introduces the individual cycles of the judges (Othniel–Samson). In other words, there is a strong connection between Judges 17–21 and Judges 1–16.[56] In Judges 1–16 we hear the repeated refrain, "The Israelites did what was evil in the sight of the Lord," while in Judges 17–21 we hear, "All the people did what was right in their own eyes" (e.g., Judg 17:6).

These two refrain-formulae "describe the same reality from two complementary viewpoints."[57] The reality communicated in the two formulae is that the absence of a king permitted people to do what they considered right in their own eyes (celebrating evil, corruption, idolatry, telling lies, stealing, dishonoring their parents, offering false offerings and consecration, practicing fear, greed, and violence, killing, and engaging in drunkenness, covetousness, and many other forms of unethical covenantal misbehavior). From a rabbinic point of view, "these events occur because of lack of leadership in Israel."[58]

Echoes of the refrain "In those days there was no king in Israel; all the people did what was right in their own eyes" (*bayyāmîm hāhēm ʾēn melek bəyîsrāʾēl, ʾîš hayyāšrār bəʿênāw yăʾăseh*) in Judges 17:6 are heard in the cries and lamentations of many Nigerian writers. For example, in Chinua Achebe's *Trouble with Nigeria*, [59] he attributes a reasonable amount of Nigeria's woes and corruption to poor leadership, comparable to the time of the judges. Mazi and Valerie Oji, along with others, agree with Chinua Achebe.

Recently, in their work *Corruption in Nigeria* (previously cited among the LCN), the Ojis acknowledge that corruption, ethical malady, moral depravity, and lack of discipline in Nigeria are connected to the poor leadership, which gradually developed when the British colonial masters withdrew

54. Olson, "Judges," 870.
55. Wilson, "As You Like It," 74.
56. Wilson, "Idolatry of Micah," 73.
57. Wilson, "Idolatry of Micah," 74.
58. Aranoff, "Idol of Micah and the Concubine at Gibeah," 78–80.
59. See Achebe, *The Trouble with Nigeria*. It's simple, popular, and readable.

from Nigeria. Oji stresses that during the internal-self-government of the three regions of Nigeria between 1954 and 1959, corruption was mildly heard of and rumored. It became stronger during the 1960s independence through the First Military Interregnum, such that it became one of the reasons for the first military coup *d'etat* of January 15, 1966, which brought General Aguyi Ironsi to power.[60] Oji further notes corruption and leadership in Nigeria, from Ironsi to General Yakubu Gowon (1967–70), from Gowon to Murtala Mohammed, and from Olusegun Obasanjo to Alhaji Shehu Shagari (1979). After Shagari came Buhari and Tunde Idiagbon, who introduced the "War Against Indiscipline" (WAI) to curb corruption in Nigeria, especially among her leaders.

Ironically, Oji also observes that the reason for General Ibrahim B. Babangida's (IBB's) coup of August 25, 1995 was Buhari's previous government's inability to control corruption in Nigeria, especially among the leaders. This explains why Babangida jettisoned WAI for Mass Mobilization for Self-Reliance, Social Justice, and Economic Recovery (MAMSAR) and Structural Adjustment Program (SAP) as soon as he came into office. In addition to these new programs, Babangida's era presided over election malpractice and the annulment of MKO Abiola's election of June 1993, as well as welcomed Chief Ernest Shoneken as an interim leader. Shenekon was removed undemocratically by General Abacha for the same reason of corruption. Abacha's government also introduced the "War Against Indiscipline and Corruption" (WAIC).

After Abacha, Nigeria had Abdusalam Abubakar, Olusegun Obasanjo, and Good Luck Jonathan before the current President, Muhamadu Burhari. Although Oji has proffered some cure for Nigerian corruption, in the rest of his work (which offers detail beyond the scope of this chapter) his points about Nigerian leadership compare with those of the Israelites during the time of the judges. Like the time of the judges, whenever "regimes came and went, the problem of (corruption) grew in its intensity 'cycles,' and pervasiveness"[61] in Nigeria. Since 1959 to date, Nigeria and its leadership remain helpless in finding a true cure for corruption, violence, kidnapping, and idolatry. Instead, many Nigerians like, the generation of Micah and his mother and other characters in the book of Judges, simply follow their own instincts, doing whatever they like. Many lack the fear of the Lord, proper

---

60. See Mazi Oji and Valerie Oji, *Corruption in Nigeria,* ix.

61. Oji, Mazi Oji and Valerie Oji, *Corruption in Nigeria,* xx.

accountability, a sense of shame, concern for the common good, and ethical responsibility.

SUMMARY

This brief exegetical-theological analysis of the morality stories about corruption and idolatry in the household shrine of Micah and his mother (Judg 17:1–6) points to some actions that can inspire African communities—Nigeria in particular—in our current context, which is dominated by all kinds of shameless corruption, violence, inordinate pursuit of wealth, ritual murder, materialism, kidnapping, idolatry, abuse of religion, tribalism, gradual collapse of family values, lack of obedience, lack of accountability, lawlessness, and the absence of selfless leadership.

These stories in *The Limits of A Divided Nation* stand as an indictment against parents, such as Micah's mother, who shy away from their responsibility of counselling their children against covetousness, reluctance to tell the truth, disunity, breaking the covenant relationship, cheating, and stealing. It was shocking that Micah's mother blessed her child rather than reproofing him (Judg 17:1–2). The same could be said of those who welcome their sons and daughters as champions—especially those who return home with looted public funds and properties.

The stories in Judges 17–21, part of which we have addressed in this chapter, invite us to critically reflect on the practices of individual congregations, denominations, and religions. Granted that the church and religious groups in our nation insist they fight corruption in many ways (through moral instruction, religious courses in schools and colleges, spiritual instruction, retreats, family catechesis, proper use of media, encyclicals and pastoral letters, magazines, journals, spiritual books, good homilies, seminars, posters, and prayer sessions, etc.),[62] to what extent do we show that these are not mere surface rhetoric, but that our actions reflect our deep knowledge of and love for God with high levels of exemplary moral integrity? In other words, stories in the book of Judges "stand as an indictment against leaders (religious, civil and traditional) who function as passive

---

62. For some documentations of the Church's fight against corruption see Udoekpo, "Chapter Four: The Liberating Mission of the Church" in *Corruption*, 33–41; Martino and Crepaldi, "Fight Against Corruption" ; Onongha, "Corruption, Culture, and Conversion," 67–82; Itebiye, "Corruption," 317–28; Editorial, "The Role of the Church."

beneficiaries of the milk of the royal cows, and neither criticize corruption and violence nor dare to console those our political classes crush."[63]

The book of Judges concludes with a statement that brackets our unit of exegesis in Judges 17:6: "In those days there was no king in Israel; the people did what was right in their own eyes" (Judg 21:25). "What was right in their own eyes" included cursing, engaging in idolatry, fighting dirty wars, engaging in violence and rape, stealing, cheating, murdering, kidnapping, and practicing all forms of corruption. What is remarkable is that God has been at work in and through this chaos of corruption, as is evident in the Deuteronomic author's choice of words. The author's use of terms like *šûbh, lāqaḥ,* and *'āśâ* suggests not only taking/stealing and returning for the purpose of "making" cultic devices, but suggests that "Micah's author teaches covenant morality at a time of corruption because he considers Israel capable of engaging in repentance, restoration, returning to the Lord, making choices that differ from those initially taken by the Micah and his mother in this story."[64]

This chapter challenges every Nigerian, as well as global readers, to ponder their actions. It encourages Nigerians to do what Micah and his mother failed to do: lament (Judg 21:3), turn to God for help, and reject all forms of corruption and idolatry.

This brings us to chapter six, where we will reflect on unity in the church-family using texts from Isaiah of Babylon and Luke.[65]

63. Onyumbe, "Interrupting Our Journeys," 269.

64. Mueller, *Morality Tale,* 127–128.

65. Some materials in this chapter were voluntarily presented as "Becoming A Church-Family in Africa That Witness the Gospel to Everyone: Perspectives from Luke 3:4–6 and Isaiah 40:4–5" at the Thirtieth Theological Conference at the Catholic Institute of West Africa(CIWA), Port Harcourt, Nigeria, April 8–12, 2019.

6

Unity from the Perspectives of Luke 3:4–6 and Isaiah 40:4–5

SCRIPTURE PORTRAYS GOD'S SAVING activity in the world in many ways.[1] Even though it is impossible to state comprehensively all that the Bible claims God is doing, it is clear that God is inclusively and without boundaries shaping a people—the Church, God's family—for himself in Christ. The message of God's unlimited mercy is heard throughout the Old Testament and New Testament.[2] It is particularly pronounced in Luke 3:5–6 and its Mosaic precursor Isaiah 40:4–5, which says, "Every valley shall be filled, and every mountain and hill shall be made low, and the crooked shall be made straight, and the rough ways made smooth; and all flesh shall see the salvation of God" (*NRSV*).

In this chapter we shall identify this church family as the people distinguished from all other human communities by faith, hope, and love, which derives from and is centered on Jesus Christ and his redemptive work.[3] Its mission derives immediately from this identity, for even by its very existence the church, as the social and historical sign of Christ's redemptive

---

1. By "Scripture" I am referring to both the Old Testament/Hebrew Bible (OT) and the New Testament (NT).

2. Recent studies that highlight this include Scobie (*Ways of Our God*, 469–651); Cazelles ("Unity of the Bible," 1–10); Deutsch ("Biblical Concept," 4–12), and Martens ("People of God," 224–253).

3. In this category belongs the Catholic Church as well as other church denominations.

work, exists in order to keep alive the memory of Jesus of Nazareth, to communicate his offer of salvation to everyone.[4]

Some of the church's challenges, blessings, and prospects have been addressed in *Ecclesia in Africa* (*EIA*), in *Africae Munus* (*AM*), by the Synod Fathers as well as in the *Instrumentum Laboris* of the Symposium of Episcopal Conference of Africa and Madagascar (SECAM), who is currently marking her Golden Jubilee.[5] Specific challenges listed in these documents include: poverty, political instability, social disorientation, war, misery, despair, and a lack of peace, justice, reconciliation, and constructive dialogue. Others challenges include division, ethnocentrism, mismanagement of ethnicity and diversity, tribalism, selfishness, kidnappings, violence, and terrorism.[6] The church-family in Africa is equally counting her many blessings, including the sacramental life of the Church, a deep sense of the sacred, of the existence of God, lively liturgy, and a cherished sense of family values. These blessings and values are ones that we hope will remain assets to the mission the church-family in Africa, which is aspiring to become a faithful, committed, united, selfless, and obedient church-family with a renewed zeal for bearing witness to Christ and reaching out to everyone. [7] Echoes of such aspirations are heard in recent interventions and the hopeful responses of several African scholars.[8]

In line with Pope Francis' spirit, these scholars are hoping for a prophetic church that goes forth into the margins—a church that is biblical, pastoral, and not self-referential, and a church that leads the way. They are

4. See Komonchack, "The Catholic University in the Church," 35.

5. See John Paul II, *Ecclesia in Africa;* Benedict XVI, *Africae Munus* and the *Instrumentum Laboris of the SECAM,* for a list of these challenges, blessings, and prospects, which include conversion, repentance, and a "renewed commitment to bearing witness to Christ."

6. Some of the basic studies I am referring to here, which have observed these challenges and prospects, include: John Paul II's *Ecclesia in Africa*, esp. nos. 39–43; Benedict XVI's *Africae Munus*; Nwachukwu, ed., *One Faith Many Tongues*. See also the publication of the Catholic Secretariat, *Church in Nigeria*.

7. See particularly *Ecclesia in Africa*, nos. 42–43.

8. Some of these interventions of African origin include those of Teresa Okure, Laurenti Magesa, Festo Mekenda, Paul Béré, Joseph G. Healey, Elian Omondi Opongo, Yvon Christian Elenga, Anthony Egan, Odomoaro Mubangizi, Anne Arabome, Ngozi Francis Uti, David Kaulem, Peter Knox, Peter Kanyandago, Nathanaël Yaovi Soédé, Michael Czenry, Paterne-Auxence Mombé, Paulinus I. Odozor, Gabriel Mmassi, and Peter J. Henriot in Orobator (ed.), *Reconciliation, Justice and Peace* and eighteen others in Orobator (ed.), *The Church We Want,* as well as Nwachukwu's *One Faith: Many Tongues,* cited above.

hoping for a church that engages in constructive dialogue, a church that is inclusive, selfless, peaceful, just, and charitable. African scholars would also like to see a church that cares for and protects its members, manages her ethnicity well, and loves and trusts its members as a loving family. They desire a church that is a servant to all, male and female alike; a church that is a voice to the voiceless, to the rich and the poor, to children and adults.

This chapter therefore intertextually and theologically studies Luke 3:4–6 and Isaiah 40:4–5. It aims to highlight the theological metaphors, hidden pastoral motifs, prophetic symbols, and missionary values of these texts—especially the ones that serve the needs of Africa and the church she longs to become. The intertextual approach adopted in this chapter presupposes, among other things, "that texts are a mosaic of earlier texts . . . texts reuse and adapt earlier texts."[9] It is "a text's representation of, reference to, and use of phenomena in the world' outside the text being interpreted."[10] In other words, "the intertexture of a text is the interaction of the language in the text with 'outside' material . . . historical events, texts, customs, values roles, institutions, and systems."[11]

This approach offers a perspective of continuity in faith and serves as reminder to the contemporary church in Africa of the corrective value of the biblical images and the theology of the church as a family, servant, herald, prophet, wilderness, voice, and way to all Africans. It attempts to illustrate the biblical and theological unity of the prophetic and salvific missions of evangelization the church-family in Africa has received from Christ. Reading it in today's era of the Pontificate of Pope Francis is also refreshing and unique. It hopes to meet the primary goal of emphasizing the role and mission of the contemporary church in Africa in light of lessons drawn from Luke 3:4–6 and Deutero-Isaiah 40:4–5.

9. Martens, "People of God," 226. Additional essays illustrating intertextuality as a method of biblical exegesis include: Martens ("Reaching for a Biblical Theology of the Whole Bible," 83–101); House ("Biblical Theology and the Wholeness of Scripture," 267–279). See also Fewell (ed.), *Reading Texts;* Hays, *Echoes of Scripture;* Brawley, *Text in Pours Forth Speech;* and Sommer, *A Prophet Reads Scriptures.*

10. Robbins, *Texture of Texts,* 40.

11. Robbins, *Texture of Texts,* 40; and Soulen and Soulen, *Handbook of Biblical Criticism,* 87–88.

UNITY AND IMAGES OF THE
CHURCH-FAMILY IN AFRICA

Various ecclesiastical documents, theological commentaries, and texts depict the church as a mystical body, a paradox, a mystery, the people of God, the temple of the Holy Spirit, the flock and sheepfold, the house in which God dwells, the bride of Christ, our mother, the holy city, and the firstfruits of the coming kingdom.[12] This chapter depicts the church as a family, the way, the wilderness, a prophet, a herald, and a servant.

Paul VI calls the family a "domestic church."[13] The family points to the "way of the Church."[14] The church-family remains the guiding principle for evangelization, or witnessing of the gospel to everyone in Africa.[15] This family mystery must continue to reflect the church in Africa, which "emphasizes care for others, solidarity, warmth in human relationship, acceptance, dialogue and trust."[16] *Africae Munus* notes that the family that the church in Africa should emulate is the "sanctuary of life."[17] It is a place that propagates the "fundamental elements of peace: justice and love between brothers and sisters."[18]

In his awareness of this ecclesial mission, which is firmly rooted in Scripture (both the OT and NT), Gerhard Lohfink points out in his *Jesus and Community: The Social Dimension of Christian Faith* that critical ecclesiology "has long asked if the historical Jesus really founded a church"[19] To Lohfink, this question must have been asked in a wrong way, "since it is not so much of an exaggeration to say that Jesus could not have found a church since there had long been one—God's people, Israel." In his view, Jesus directed his effort to Israel and sought to gather it in view of the coming of

12. For some of these debates on the meaning and nature of the church, see Lubac, *Church: Paradox and Mystery*; Vatican II, *Lumen Gentium,* no. 21; *Gaudium et Spes*, no. 7.

13. *Evangelii Nuntiandi*, no. 71.

14. Pope John Paul II, *Familiaris Cosortio*, no. 15.

15. *Ecclesia in Africa*, nos. 63–64. Also Pope Francis (*Lumen Fidei,* no. 52 and *Evangelii Gaudium*, no. 66) sees the connection between the family and faith.

16. See John Paul II's *Ecclesia in Africa*, no. 63; and Benedict the XVI's *Africae Munus*, nos.7–9.

17. *Africae Munus*, no. 42.

18. *Africae Munus*, no. 43.

19. Lohfink, *Jesus and Community,* xi.

the reign of God and to make it into the true people of God, sanctified by his death.[20]

Charles Scobie's work *The Ways of Our God: An Approach to Biblical Theology* (2003) echoes Lohfink's remarks. In it, Scobie observes:

> Recognition of "the people of God" as a major biblical theme does not depend in any narrow sense on the use of a particular terminology, but rather in the broadest possible way on the fact that the "story line" of salvation history (*heilsgeshcichte*), is largely the account of relations between God and Israel in the OT and God and the church in the NT.[21]

The Old Testament describes Israel as a "people" (*'am* in the *MT*; and *Laos* in the *LXX*) chosen by God from among the nations (*gôyîm; ethnē* in the *LXX*). The actual phrase "people of God" occurs only eleven times, but phrases such as "my people," "your people," and "his people" occur frequently (about 300 times).[22]

Israel's story as God's people begins with the call of the individual Abraham in Genesis 12:1–3. God brings Abraham and his descendants, the "children of Israel" (*bǝnêyisrā'ēl*), into being. Related terms used to describe them are *qāhāl* and *'ēdhāh*. *Qāhāl* translates as "congregation" or "assembly," referring to a group of people gathered for a purpose, such as battle (1 Sam 17:47), entering into a covenant (such as at Mount Sinai), or for worship (Ps 22:22). *'Ēdhāh* relates an assembly or gathering and stresses corporate unity. In the *LXX qāhāl* translates *ekklēsia*, while *'ēdhāh* translates *synagōgē*, and never as *ekklēsia*.[23]

It is in the story of this assembly, Israel, that we find the roots of the church as the people of God, a chosen and elected people *(bāchar)*, a congregation, a covenant community (Gen 9:1–17; 15; 17; Exod 19–24; 2 Sam 7; 23:5; Ps 89:3, 28; 1 Kgs 8:23–22; Jer 33:21), the faithful remnant, leading to the renewed Israel of the New Testament.[24] In other words, the Bible is concerned with the relationship between God and people of all walks of life, including Africans. Notably, with the birth of Christ, that relationship continues in the New Testament and fulfils the promises made to Abraham and his descendants (Luke 1:54–55).

20. Lohfink, *Jesus and Community*, xi.
21. Scobie, *Ways of Our God*, 469.
22. Scobie, *Ways of Our God*, 469.
23. Scobie, *Ways of Our God*, 470.
24. See details in Scobie's *Ways of Our God*, 470–486.

Bender, in his work *These Are My People: The Nature of the Church and Its Disciples According to the New Testament*, speaks of this church as the body of Christ, which is called to respond to God's gracious acts.[25] Okure describes this church as the community of believers (including the Church), humanity, and the entire creation (2 Cor 5:19; Col 1:20, Eph 1:10; John 11:52; 12:32).[26] She further sees the New Testament church, in light of Pope Francis, as the church that comes alive when lived and witnessed by going forth (Matt 28:16–20) to the poor and the marginalized.[27]

Minear's work *Images of the Church in the New Testament* lists about ninety-six analogies of the church.[28] These are in addition to the one we find in Avery Dulles's *Models of the Church.*[29] Most significant for us is the basic principle of the Synod and SECAM Fathers—namely, the Church as a family of God's people.[30] This principle is based, in part, in the ministry of Jesus, who said in Matthew 12:50, "Whoever does the will of my Father in heaven is my brother and sister and mother." Mark 10:28–30 teaches that Christ's disciples have to make sacrifices, perhaps leaving their natural families, but they gain a new family of "brothers and sisters, mothers and children." Above all, in Galatians 6:10, believers are "those of the family of faith (*tous oikeious tēs pisteōs*)." They are children of God, their Father, and thus brothers and sisters of one another (Rom 16:1; 1 Cor 7:15; Jas 2:15).This is God's family of faith, the church in Africa that Africans yearn to fully become. The role of this church-family, as a community without boundaries, a community for all, a prophet, a herald, the way, a wilderness, and a servant, as viewed in relation to Luke 3 4–6 and Isaiah 40:4–5, deserves further attention.

---

25. See Bender, *These Are My People,* 14–66.

26. Okure, "Church-Family of God," 13–24.

27. Okure, "Becoming the Church of the New Testament," 93–105.

28. See Minear, *Images of the Church.*

29. See Avery Cardinal Dulles, *Models of the Church,* expanded edition (New York: Doubleday, 2002), where listed images include the church as institution, mystical communion, sacrament, herald, servant, eschatology, and true church.

30. See also Lohfink, *Jesus and Community,* 39–44.

UNITY AND PERSPECTIVES FROM LUKE 3:4–6

Luke's Gospel is one of the treasures of biblical literature.[31] Christologically, it presents Jesus not only as the Son of God, a prophet, the Lord of history, the Messiah, and the Son of Man, but also as the redeemer and savior of the world. Luke 3:1–6 contains prophetic allusions and draws some symbols, motifs, and images from Mark and Deutero-Isaiah. With these borrowings, Luke offers the church in Africa something to think about in their role as the way, a wilderness, a prophet, and a family to all people. Luke historically presents John the Baptist as an eschatological prophet similar to Elijah (cf. Luke 1:16–17). In Luke 3:1–2a Luke fixes the date of John's calling. In Luke 3:2b he describes the call of John, and in Luke 3:3 he identifies the place of John's ministry.

In Luke 3:4–6 Luke presents John's ministry as a fulfilment of Scripture:

> 4 As it is written in the book of the words of the prophet Isaiah, "the voice of one crying out in the wilderness: prepare the way of the Lord, make his path straight. 5 Every valley shall be filled, and every mountain and hill shall be made low, and the crooked shall be made straight, 6 and the rough ways made smooth; and all flesh shall see the salvation of God. (*NRSV*)

Echoes of this Lukan passage are heard in Mark 1:1, which introduces John the Baptist as a prophet who came to prepare the way for the Lord. John successfully prepared the Lord's way by baptizing all people (Luke 3:21; Mark 1:5; Matt 1:5). Luke intertextually adapts and reuses Mark to make his theological points concerning John the Baptist. First, he creatively moves Mark 1:2, the quotation from Malachi 3:1, to another place in Luke 7:27, and then positions Deutero-Isaiah's quotation of Mark 1:3 (Isa 40:3) after his introduction of John's ministry (Luke 3:4). Luke is then left with Mark 1:4, which he shifts to another place in Luke 3:3b and then adds "the word of God came to John son of Zechariah in the wilderness" (Luke 3:2b).

Luke is interested in stressing three things: First, he stresses the prophetic dimension of John the Baptist, the prophet (*nābî'*). Second, he stresses the theological significance of the place of his ministry as "in the wilderness" (*en tē erēmōi*), a phrase that he repeats elsewhere (Luke 1:80; 3:2b), including Luke 3:4: "the voice of one crying out in the wilderness" (*phōnē boōvtos en tē erēmōi*). Third, Luke stresses the content of the

---

31. R. Allen Culpepper, "The Gospel of Luke: Introduction, Commentary, and Reflections," *NIBC* 8, ed. Leander E. Keck (Nashville: Abingdon Press, 2015), 3.

ministry of John the Baptist as a tireless prophet. A prophet speaks on behalf of another, especially a deity.[32] Israel's prophets were divinely called to preach and interpret the covenant theology of God's people, of their time and culture.[33] While engaging in this mission, they remained sensitive to evil (Amos 8:4–8; Jer 2:12–13).[34] A prophet recognizes the importance of trivialities, is luminous and explosive, pursues the highest good, and practices austerity and compassion. The biblical prophets make sure that few are guilty while all are responsible. A prophet is like a blast from heaven that faces a coalition of callousness and authority and embraces loneliness and misery. A prophet is a messenger, God's partner and associate.[35]

From the perspective of Luke, John the Baptist is a prophet, God's messenger and his associate. The church in Africa, like John ,must be prophetic in her mission. This same message is heard in *Ecclesia in Africa* and *Africae Munus*. In these documents, the Synod Fathers, like the Evangelist Luke, invites the church-family in Africa to review her prophetic mission of justice and peace, dialogue and reconciliation, family values, and gospel inculturation, simplicity of life, caring for the planet, courage and compassion in evangelization, and selflessness in reaching out to the poor with a sense patriotism and common good.

Luke's emphasis on the place of John's ministry, "in the wilderness" (*en tē erēmōi*), also offers a message for the Church in Africa. He suggests that there is still room to work hard to become that church-family in the wilderness Christ expects of her. Wilderness is used here symbolically, as is common in biblical tradition.[36] The Torah sometimes portrays the wilderness (*midbār/erēmos*) as a place of testing. It is a place where life's necessities are not sufficient (Num 14:26–35; Deut 9:7).[37]

---

32. See Udoekpo, *Israel's Prophets*, 2–3; Anderson, *Understanding the Old Testament*, 248.

33. Wifall, *Israel's Prophets*, 12.

34. See Udoekpo, *Israel's Prophets*, 5; Heschel, *Prophets*, 1–31.

35. See Heschel, *Prophets*, 3–31; Udoekpo, *Israel's Prophets*, 5.

36. See Acts of the Apostles 7:36–44; Shemaryahu ("The Desert Motif," 31–63); Baker ("Wilderness, Desert," 893–97); Archie ("Wilderness," 848–854); Funk ("The Wilderness," 205–214); and Schofield ("Wilderness," 1337), where it is noted that "literarily and symbolically, the wilderness has been an important backdrop for the development of Jewish identity. From early biblical narratives, frequently set in the wilderness, to Second Temple literature, the wilderness becomes a theologically charged image, (re)used and thematized by various Jewish groups."

37. See Burnett, "Eschatological Prophet of Restoration," 1–24.

In the prophetic books, Hosea sees the desert (*midbār/erēmos* /wilderness) as the place of God's covenant renewal with his people, Israel.[38] Africans hope for a better tomorrow from their own "deserts" of insufficient food, water, light, good roads, stable democracy, rule of law, good leadership, freedom of worship, and other fundamental human rights.

In Luke's Gospel, "wilderness" has a positive connotation as a place where prophets are called for a deeper encounter with God (Luke 1:80; 3:2; 4:42; 5:16). The prophetic church-family in Africa and her agents of evangelization (Bishops, priests, religious people, consecrated persons, catechists, and lay faithful) are invited into a deeper relationship with Christ.[39]

Luke's use of the wilderness motif also strengthens his prophetic portrait of John. He links John with Moses and Elijah, both of whom received their calling in the desert (Exod 3; 1 Kgs 19:4–18). In Luke, the seemingly inhospitable desert is meant to highlight the hope and sufficiency of a new exodus, the way of the Lord, the eschatological renewal of God's people occurring in the wilderness.[40] Again, in Luke's view, John is an itinerant preacher of the baptism of repentance for the forgiveness of sin (Luke 3:3b). Baptism for him is the outward sign of repentance (Luke 3:8, 10–14). It is a sign of total surrendering to God and of the gathering of everyone into that universal family of God's children, including the church-family in Africa.

LUKE'S USE OF 2 ISAIAH 40:3–5 (LXX)

In addition to Luke's portrayal of John as a prophet called to preach the baptism of repentance in the wilderness, Luke appeals to Isaiah 40:3–5, which says:

> 3 A voice crying out in the wilderness/desert, prepare the way of the Lord! Make straight in the wasteland a highway for our God. 4 every valley shall be filled in, every mountain and hill shall be made a plain, the rough country, a broad valley. 5 Then the glory of the Lord shall be revealed, and all people/flesh mankind shall see it together, for the mouth of the Lord has spoken. (NAB; *LXX*)[41]

---

38. *HALOT* 2.546–547.

39. See list of this invited agent of evangelization in *Ecclesia in Africa*, nos. 88–98.

40. Burnett, *Eschatological Prophet*, 9.

41. (v.3) *Phōnē boōntos en tē erēmō hetoimasate ten hodon kuriou eutheias poieite tas tribous tou theou hemōn* (v.4) *pasa pharagxh plērōthēsetai kai pan oros kai bounos tapeinōthēsetai kai estai panta ta skolia eis eutheian kai hē tracheia eis pedia* (v.5) *kai*

Luke uses this text differently than Mark. He omits most of Mark's introduction and extends Isaiah's quotation (Isa 40:3) in Mark 1:2 to Isaiah 40:3–5 in Luke 3:4–6, which "anticipates and clarifies the activities of John." [42] Such activities are close to the heart of the church-family in Africa throughout this chapter. Deutero-Isaiah 40:1–11 bears the essence of the prophet's universal message of salvation, reused by Luke. [43] It reflects a human journey, but God's coming and presence dominates, which is relevant for the church-family in Africa.

Isaiah 40:1–11 highlights the following facts:

1. The exiles are to take heart because their sins have now been expiated and their term of punishment over (Isa 40:1–2).

2. The Lord is about to come to his people's aid in such a decisive fashion that the whole world will be amazed at the revelation of his glory (Isa 40:3–5).

3. The guarantee of this message of hope, comfort, and restoration is the word of the Lord spoken through the prophet, which is all powerful and tremendously important when compared with all human activity (Isa 40:6–8). [44]

Isaiah 40:3–5 in particular is filled with promises of covenant restoration for the people. Even though the Israelites have been exiled in Babylon (Isa 39), this ordeal will not last. The Israelites shall be redeemed and comforted (Isa 40:2). There will be another exodus beginning with a voice crying for the construction of a highway from Babylon to Judah, through the impassable Arabian Desert. [45] This highway will not be like others; it will level the hills and mountains, reveal God's greatness, and bring salvation to people of all nations (Isa 40:3–5).

---

ophthēsetai he doxa kuriou kai ophetai pasa sarxh to sōtērion tou theou hoti kurios elalēsen.

42. Koet, "Isaiah In Luke-Acts," 79–100.

43. In Webb (*Message of Isaiah;* 161) it is noted also that "this opening part of chapter 40 is like the overture to a great musical composition." Major themes found here include (v. 1) comfort, (v. 2) atonement, (v. 3) the way of the Lord, (v. 4) the glory of the Lord, (v. 5) the power of the Word of God, (v. 8ff) the city of God, (v. 9) and the might and tenderness of Zions savior (vv. 10–11).

44. See Whybray (*Second Isaiah,* 45) for this central message of Deutero-Isaiah.

45. For this geographic characterization, see Branick, *Understanding the Prophets,* 192.

We should note that different texts offer different locations for the voice of Isaiah 40:3. In the Masoretic Text, the Dead Sea Scrolls, and the Targumim of Isaiah, the location is in the wilderness—namely, "a voice cries, in the wilderness."(*qōl qōrē' bamidbar*).[46] In the *LXX* of Isaiah, closely followed by Luke, the voice is "crying out in the wilderness" (*Phōnē boōntos en tē erēmō*), prepare the way for the Lord (*hetoimasate ten hodon kuriou*). Commenting on this, Joseph Fitzmyer suggests that since the new exodus did not materialize in the second temple Judaism as humanly expected, Luke the historian concluded that the wait was over and that John is "the voice of one crying out in the wilderness" (v. 3b).[47]

That Luke identifies John as preaching in the wilderness (*en tē erēmō/ midbār*) is significant for the church-family in Africa. As suggested by the SECAM Bishops, it is a place of repentance and conversion as well as a place of renewed commitment to bearing witness to Christ.[48] It is a place for learning how to endure testing in the midst of poverty, deficient democracy, disunity, management of ethnicity, and strife to cultivate a genuine spirit of disposition in encountering a merciful God, with the hope for a better future.

In addition, we must emphasize the relevance of the phrase "prepare the way of the Lord" (*hetoimasate ten hodon kuriou*). First, this phrase functions as a pointer to the infancy narrative of the Gospel, where the angel Gabriel prophesied that John will prepare (*etaoimasai*) a people for the Lord (Luke 1:17). Zechariah, filled with the Holy Spirit, also says in Luke 1:76 that John will "prepare his way" (*etomasai hodous autou*). Second, it looks forward through the Gospel and projects into the Acts of the Apostle, where we find the early Christians being referred to as the people of "the way" (*derek/hodos*, Acts 9:2; 18:25; 19:9, 23; 24:14, 22).[49]

These functions project the very concept of evangelization, which is familiar to us. For example, *Lineamenta for the First National Pastoral Congress* (in Nigeria) states that "evangelization was the task Jesus entrusted to his Church at the point of his departure from this world to return to his

46. See commentary on in Burnette, "Eschatological Prophets," 15.

47. Fitzmyer, *The Gospel According to Luke*, 461.

48. SECAM, *Instrumentum Laboris*, 3–4.

49. See Blenkinsopp (*Isaiah 1–39*, 181–84) where he suggests that "the use of *derek* as a group designation is admittedly not so clear in Qumran as *hodos* is in Acts, but usage in the various rules favours that conclusion; the members are 'the elect of the way' (1QS IX 17–18) and 'the perfect way' (1QMXIV 7), while recidivists are those who 'deviate from the way' (CD 1 13; II 16)."

Father."[50] Jesus mandated his apostles to "Go therefore, make disciples of all nations; baptize them in the name of the Father and of the Son and of the Holy Spirit, and teach them to observe all the commands" (Matt 28:19–20; Mark 16:15).

Pope Paul VI stresses that evangelization means:

> bringing the Good News into all the strata of humanity, and through its influence transforming humanity from within, and making it new; "Now I am making the whole of creation new." (Rev 21:5; 2 Cor 5:17; Gal 6:15) ... The purpose of evangelization is therefore precisely this interior change, and if it had to be expressed in one sentence the best way of stating it would be to say that the Church evangelizes when she seeks to convert, solely through the divine power of the Message she proclaims, both the personal and collective consciences of the people, the activities in which they engage, and the lives and concrete milieu which are theirs.[51]

The Church in Africa must lead the "Way" of Christ to people, and it must lead people to Christ in various ways through various agents, characterized by peace, justice, reconciliation, dialogue, unity, communalism, moral teaching, media, and inculturation.[52] In this light, *Africae Munus* describes the Church in Africa as a "sentinel" or a "watchman."[53] As the way, a watchman, or a sentinel, the Church in Africa "feels the duty to be present wherever human suffering exists and to make heard the silent cry of the innocent who suffer persecution, or of peoples whose government mortgage their present and the future for personal interests."[54]

This vocation and mission of the church-family requires humility and docility in spirit. It requires the type of docility we see in the Suffering Servant of God of Second Isaiah, from which Luke draws. Like the Suffering Servant of Second Isaiah, the church-family in Africa must see herself as a leader-servant. She must continue to sing the four songs of the Suffering Servant of Yahweh, individually and collectively (cf. Isa 42:1–4; 49:1–16;

50. Catholic Secretariat, *Church in Nigeria*, 19.

51. Pope Paul VI, *Evangeilli Nuntiandi*, no. 18.

52. *Africae Munus* nos. 99–131, lists these agents to include: bishops, priests, missionaries, permanent deacons, consecrated persons, seminarians, catechists, and lay people. This is in addition to the Holy Spirit, the church, and family listed in *Ecclesia in Africa*, no. 92 and in the *Church in Nigeria: Family of God on Mission*, nos. 34–39.

53. *Africae Munus*, no. 30.

54. *Africae Munus*, no. 30.

50:4–9; 52:13–53:12). Such music is in line with the very concept of election, with which we began this chapter. Election, as cited by Scobie, comes with a responsibility.[55] Election as it relates to the "the notion of a people of God is never a claim to superiority but rather a call to service."[56] Abraham and his descendants, as we noted, were blessed in Genesis 12:2, so that they in turn could be a blessing to others. It is the church-family's vocation to be of service to humanity.

Avery Dulles has commented extensively on this servant model of the Church.[57] He writes:

> The Church is the body of Christ, the suffering servant, and hence the servant of the Church. "So it is that the Church announces the coming of the Kingdom not only in word, through preaching and proclamation, but more particularly in work, in her ministry of reconciliation, of binding up wounds, of suffering service, of healing . . . And the Lord was the 'man for others,' so must the Church be 'the community for others.' "[58]

In addition to all this, the Church in Africa must continue to pay close attention to the universal story of salvation in Luke 3:5 and Isaiah 40:4–5, which is directed to "all flesh" (*pasa sarx, kol-bāśār*). Intertextually, we notice that starting in Luke 3:5, Luke departs from Mark. Luke prefers to lengthen Isaiah's quotation from Isaiah 40:3 to Isaiah 40:5.

He closely follows the *LXX* of Isaiah 40, with few changes.[59] He omits "all" (*panta*) from his quotation and alters the singular noun "rough way" or "country" (*tracheia*) to the plural "rough ways" (*tracheiai*). Luke also deletes "plain" (*eis pedia*) and inserts "smooth ways" (*eis hodous leias*), affirming his fondness for the way.[60]

Rhetorically, the church-family in Africa is facing its own challenges of levelling rough or the crooked ways, filling in valleys, and bringing low mountains. The rough spots and valleys are neutralized and eliminated not only by the presence of God in her midst, but in the humble evangelizing and prophetic missions of the Church. David Balch suggests that this valley and mountain imagery be viewed as a fulfilment of the *Magnificat*, where

55. Scobie, *Ways of our God*, 472.

56. Shaw, *Pilgrim People of God*, 8.

57. See Dulles, "The Church as Servant," *Models of the Church*, 81–113.

58. Dulles, *Models of the Church*, 85.

59. See details of this in Burnett, "Eschatological Prophet," 17.

60. Burnette, "Eschatological Prophet," 18.

the Lord "scattered the proud," " brought down the powerful," "filled the hungry with good things," and "sent away the rich empty handed" (Luke 1:51–53).[61]

As Luke sums up his use of Isaiah 40:3–5, he omits the phrase "the glory of the Lord shall appear" (*kai ophthēsetai hē doxa kuriou*) from Isaiah 40:5, perhaps because in his view the glory of the Lord is near. For him, with the prophetic role of John, the glory of the long-awaited savior is near. Luke thereafter uses the remaining section of Isaiah word-for word: "and all flesh shall see the salvation of God" (*kai ophtai pasa sarx to sotērion tou theou*).[62] For Isaiah, the oppressed, whether in exile in Babylon or scattered throughout ravished Judah, are not just part of all flesh, they are a covenant people. Many have observed that "one of the clearest rationales for Luke's extension of the Isaiah quotation is visible with Isaiah's universal emphasis on divine salvation to all flesh and mankind" whose preaching is entrusted as well to the church-family in Africa.[63] It's a reminder of Simeon, who, when taking the baby Jesus, proclaims him as "the salvation" (*to sōtērion*) of God that has been prepared for "all peoples, a light for revelation to the Gentiles and for the glory of your people Israel" (Luke 2:30–32).[64]

This has led to Culpepper's evaluation that "Luke's most dramatic insight is his perception that Jesus announced salvation for all people alike."[65] In Luke, God sent Elisha and Elijah to a widow in Sidon and to a leper from Syria (Luke 4:24–30), territories outside Israel. In Luke, God's mercy knows no bounds. It reaches to those from the east, west, north, and south (Luke 13:29). God's Son, the Christ of Luke, sent his disciples to inclusively preach to all nations (Luke 24:47; Acts 1:8). He gives the church-family in Africa a template for outreach to sinners, Samaritans, tax collectors, men, women, outcasts, the poor, and the rich. He gives a template to upset "through the power of the Gospel, mankind's criteria of judgment, determining values, points of interest, lines of thoughts, sources of inspiration and models of life which are contrast with the Word of God and the plan of salvation."[66]

---

61. Balch, "*Luke*," 1110.

62. See, Burnette, "Eschatological Prophet," 18.

63. See Meek, *Gentile Mission,* 20; Nolland, *Luke,* 138.

64. Mallan, *Reading and Transformation of Isaiah in Luke-Acts,* 71. In fact, notice it is only as the narrative of Luke-Acts unfolds that this promise comes to fruition as the gospel is taken to Jews, Samaritans and Gentiles (Acts 1:8; 2–7; 8; 10–11; 15).

65. Culpepper, "Luke," 16.

66. *Evangelii Nuntiandi,* no. 19.

Christ also gives the church-family in Africa a template for dialogue and listening, as he listens "not simply those who would tell him what he would like to hear."[67] Of course, this is the church Pope Francis prefers. He also prefers a church that is "living in the midst of the homes of the sons and daughters."[68] He prefers a church that is "in contact with the homes and lives of its people, and does not become a useless structure out of touch with people or a self-absorbed cluster made up of a chosen few."[69] He prefers a church-family in Africa that "'goes forth' and whose doors are open to everyone."[70]

SUMMARY

We can draw several conclusions from our discussion in this chapter. First, we can conclude that the church-family in Africa is not only faced with many challenges, blessings, and prospects, but is still growing into becoming that which Christ commanded. Second, we can conclude that the church-family in Africa is invited to become the way, the sentinel, the watchman, a prophet, and a servant leader in the likes of the Suffering Servant of Deutero-Isaiah and John the Baptist. She is invited to promote unity and to become an agent of evangelization who witnesses the gospel to everyone, poor and rich alike, irrespective of gender, culture, sociopolitical class, or geographical boundaries. And finally, we can conclude that the church-family in Africa must draw lessons from Isaiah 40 4–5 and Luke 3:4–6 and its rich metaphors, symbols, images, and theology of the church as family, servant, herald, prophet, wilderness, the voice, and the way to salvation for all Africans.

In the following chapter, we will discuss unity from the Pauline perspective related in Romans 14–15.

---

67. *Evangelii Gaudium*, no. 31.

68. *Evangelii Gaudiium*, no. 28.

69. *Evangelii Gaudium*, no. 28.

70. *Evangelii Gaudium*, nos.43–47; see also Udoekpo, *Pope Francis*, 81–86.

7

Unity from the Perspectives of Romans 14:1–15:13

THROUGHOUT SCRIPTURE THERE IS a sustained emphasis on the fact that if people truly know and love God, then they must walk in his ways and maintain good relationships with fellow believers. The biblical ethics of unity, of welcoming and tolerating one another, both weak and strong, which we hear especially in Romans 14:1–15:13, can be challenging for the church-family in Africa. The Roman community Paul addressed in this letter was facing such challenges as misunderstandings, disunity between "the weak" and "the strong," disunity between Jews and Gentiles, a lack of tolerance for others people's observance, as well as a refusal to imitate Christ. We see similar challenges in today's pluralistic contexts across African nations and beyond. Many of these challenges have already been examined in *Ecclesia in Africa* (EIA), in *Africae Munus* (AM), and in the *Instrumentum Laboris of the Symposium of Episcopal Conference of Africa and Madagascar* (SECAM), and they are the focus of this work as well.

As mentioned in previous chapters, Africa faces challenges including disunity, a lacking sense of common good, political instability, poor leadership, proliferation of worship centers, social disorientation, war, misery, despair, lack of peace, justice, and dialogue. Many African nations also experience division, ethnocentrism, and mismanagement of ethnicity, violence, tribalism, and lack tolerance for one another.[1]

---

1. See *Ecclesia in Africa*, nos. 42–43; *Africae Munus*; *Secam Instrumentum Laboris*,

This chapter builds on the material presented in previous chapters. It offers an analysis of the "lack of ethics of tolerance for one another's observance" in Romans 14:1–15:13 from a theologically, metaphorical, and sociopolitical perspective. That is, this chapter focuses on the need for believers, "the weak" and "the strong," to learn to live side by side in peace in the church-family in Africa.

Before we begin our analysis, we must offer clarification on a few points—namely, (1) Paul's reason for writing his letter to the Romans, (2) a working identity and nature of "the weak" and "the strong," and (3) some relevant images of the church-family in Africa.

The approach we'll take in this chapter is not only refreshing, especially in today's era of the papacy of Pope Francis, a widely received global religious leader, but it also reminds us in our varied contexts of the true relationship between the gospel and life. It also reminds us of the ethical imperative to always welcome one another, to treat people with Christ's love, and to tolerate our neighbors, "the weak" and "the strong," irrespective of their culture, gender, religion, or sociopolitical class (John 13:15; Rom 15:1–3).

WHY PAUL WROTE THE LETTER TO THE ROMANS

Paul's letter to the Romans is the first and the longest of Paul's letters in the New Testament. It offers the most detailed description of Paul's gospel and has great influence on Christian theology. In fact, it has been described as Paul's masterpiece that "dwarfs most of his other writings, an Alpine peak towering over hills and villages."[2] Scholars are of the opinion that in order to understand why Paul wrote Romans, a letter that remains relevant to the Church in Africa, we need to step back into the historical circumstances of Paul and of the Romans.[3] This is what Taylor Jr., intends to do by suggesting that we seek answers for the following three questions:

1. How was the community founded?

2. How did the edict of Claudius affect the community?

3–5; Achebe, *Trouble with Nigeria;* and Nwachukwu, *One Faith Many Tongues.*

2. Matera, *Romans,* 3; Wright, *Letter to the Romans,* 319.

3. These scholars and their opinions are found in Donfried, *Romans Debates;* Byrne, *Romans.*

3. What kind of people made up the community to whom Paul wrote?[4]

Similar questions are worth contemplating by members of the church-family in a pluralistic Africa who seek to welcome and tolerate one another in imitation of Christ ,who first welcomed all.

As if anticipating Walter's proposal, Matera opines that Paul's wrote this letter from Corinth, from the home of Gaius, during the winter and spring of AD 56; that Paul completed his work in the East with the intention of opening a mission in Spain. On his journey to Spain, he planned to visit the Christ-believers in Rome. But prior to this, he needed to bring the collection that he had taken up among the Gentile congregation to the poor Christ-believers in Jerusalem.[5]

Matera also notes that Christianity came to Rome before Paul wrote to the Romans. While the original believers may have been converts from Judaism, there was a large Gentile contingent in Rome at the time Paul wrote. These Roman Christians, like the African Christians discussed in *Ecclesia in Africa,* "belonged to different households' churches, in which there may have been tensions between Jewish Christians and the law-observant Gentile Christians, on the one hand, and Gentiles believers who did not observe the law, on the other. While the latter group was probably sympathetic to Paul's gospel, the former was probably wary of the apostle's teaching." [6]

Based on Taylor Jr., and Matera's proposals, we can conclude that Paul wrote Romans for the following reasons:

1. to summarize his gospel

2. to prepare the Romans for his visit to Rome

3. to ask them to support his new missionary work in Spain

4. to resolve any misgivings about his understanding of the gospel and to prevent inroads by missionaries who disagreed with him

5. to ask for prayers for his trip to Jerusalem and possibly intercession with Jerusalem believers

6. to resolve the problem of the weak and the strong—that is, the problem of disunity.[7]

4. See Taylor Jr., *Paul,* 229.

5. Matera, *Romans,* 6.

6. Ibid., 8.

7. These are all collaborated by Matera, *Romans,* 8; Taylor Jr., *Paul,* 235; Wedderburn, *Reasons for Romans,* 140–142; Fitzmyer, *Romans;* and Cranfield, *Romans.*

But who are "the weak" and "the strong" for Paul, and for the Church in Africa and beyond?

WORKING IMAGES OF "THE WEAK" AND "THE STRONG"

While most commentators agree that Romans 14:1–15:13 is an exhortation that focuses on the relationship between the weak and the strong, there is disagreement on the exact nature and identity of "the weak" and "the strong." While most argue that "the weak" were Jewish Christians who observed the dietary and ritual prescriptions of the law, and "the strong" were Gentile Christians who found no need to do so, others assess the ethnic makeup of this group differently. [8] Andrew Das, for example, argues that both the weak and the strong were Gentile Christians. The former had a deep appreciation of Judaism and its practices because they had been closely associated with the synagogue, whereas the latter did not. [9] The underlying issue, Taylor Jr. argues, is disagreement over food rules and holy days. Some members of the community abstained from certain foods and observed holy days not observed by the whole believing community. They were probably "the weak" (Rom 14:1). Moreover, the "strong" (probably those who agree with Paul) are to support and carry along the weak (Rom 15:1).[10]

Given Paul's teachings on "the weak" and "the strong," let's apply this passage to the church Africa. In Africa, how often do we judge one another based on tribe, color, gender, food and drink choices, schools attended, degrees acquired, style of dress, socioeconomic status, and language? How often do we inordinately discriminate against others because of their religion, region, state, local government, clan, village, family, culture, church denomination, or political party? It is from the perspectives of oneness and unity that the metaphors of the "weak" and the "strong" are used in this book for the church-family in Africa, whose identity we must continue to affirm.

We have already identified the church-family in Africa in the preceding chapter. We can only reaffirm here that there are many images found in ecclesiastical documents, theological treatises, and literature that are relevant for our discussion. These documents portray the church as the

8. For details see Matera, *Romans*, 306.

9. See Das, *Solving the Romans Debate*, 264.

10. Taylor Jr., *Paul*, 248.

mystical body, a paradox, a mystery, the people of God, the temple of the Holy Spirit, the flock and sheepfold, the house in which God dwells, the bride of Christ, our mother, the holy city. and the firstfruits of the coming kingdom.[11]

But the image of the church as "a family" remains most relevant for us thanks to Paul VI, who encourages us to see the family as "a domestic Church." [12]

John Paul II reminds us that it is the family that points the "way of the Church."[13] The Church must remain the guiding principle for evangelization, which includes welcoming the weak and the strong into the church-family in Africa.[14] This church-family must emphasize care for others, solidarity, warmth in human relationships, acceptance, dialogue, trust, and unity. It must be a "sanctuary of life" for all as well as a place that propagates the "fundamental elements of peace, justice, and love between brothers and sisters, as preached by Paul in Romans 14:1–15:13.[15]

ETHICAL IMPLICATIONS OF ROMANS 14:1–15:13 FOR AFRICA

In the final part of Romans, Paul presents his readers, including the Church in Africa, with an extended exhortation in which he urges them to live a morally good life made possible by the saving righteousness that God has manifested in Christ's death and resurrection. This section on the transformed life of believers has two major units. The first unit is on humility, love, obedience, and service among believers (Rom 12:1–13:14). The second unit, which we will focus on (Rom 14:1–15:13), is an invitation for people of all walks of life, customs, and ethnic identities to live in unity, tolerating one another without judgement (Rom 14:1–12).

While adjudicating between two factions that he identifies as "the strong" (*hoi dynatoi*) and "the weak" (*ta asthenēmata*), Paul exhorts the Roman Christians not to judge or scandalize one another because of

---

11. See De Lubac (*Church, Lumen Gentium, Gaudium et Spes*); Bender (*Nature of the Church*, 14–66); Okure ("Church-Family of God," 13–24; "Church of the NT," 93–105); Minear (*Images of the Church*); and Dulles (*Models*).

12. *Evangelii Nuntiandi*, no. 71.

13. *Familiaris Consortio*, no. 15.

14. For further emphasis see *Ecclesia in Africa*, nos. 63–64.

15. See *Africae Munus*, no. 42.

differing opinions regarding diet and the observance of particular days, but to sustain and receive one another (*proslambanesthe allēlous*) as Christ has received them (Rom 15:7–13). Romans 14:1–4 in particular is a true reminder that in Africa, even though saving faith may lead us to abstain from certain things—especially certain food, drinks, customs, and cultural elements—doing so does not ethically determine our standing before God. Loving families do accommodate members of the family who are allergic to certain food items and drinks, and so should the church-family in Africa.

In Romans 14:5–9 Paul deals with another issue causing division: considering particular days more sacred than others. In is context, the days causing division were probably the Jewish Sabbath and other festivals.[16] Paul's exhortation in this regard applies to the Church in Africa in relation to what they do or do not do on Sundays and Holy Days of obligations. These days in the Church in Africa does not prohibit love and acts of charity, or acts of saving our neighbors' lives, especially by health workers in clinics and hospitals. For Paul, judgment should be left to God alone (Rom 14:10–12).

In addition, Christians even when they think they are free and right, must not be a source of scandal to others. They must live in unity without offending others (Rom 14:13–23). The strong should not condemn the weak by insisting on their convictions about dietary prescriptions. Like in Paul's days, some believers today in Africa are uncaring; they use their freedom not only to cause their neighbors to stumble, but they are also offensive.

Whether we are strong and insensitive to others, or weak and petty about trivial things (e.g., food, style of dress, drink, ones' village of origin, or dialect, whether Hausa, Yoruba, Igbo, Efik, Annang, Ibibio, Ogoni, Oron, Ogoja, or Ijaw and Ikwere, etc.), we can become the reason that fellow believers fall into sin. Paul reminds members of the Church in Africa that it is unethical to cause problems for others (Rom 14:14–16). On the contrary, members of the Church in Africa are to serve Christ by tolerating others and maintaining peace in the workplace, institutions, and in religious and civil communities. In other words, what is important for God's kingdom is not food and drink, nor where we come from, but righteousness, peace, harmony, tolerance, and joy in the Holy Spirit (Rom 14:17–19, 20–21).

In Romans 14:22–23 Paul offers the church-family in Africa, three pieces of advice:

---

16. For details, see Kasali, "Romans," 1349–76.

1. We should not voice our opinions indiscriminately when we know that they may offend other members of the family. This does not mean we should not speak up, but we must do so at the right time and place and in manner that will build up the community.

2. In all that we do, we must not be against our conscience.

3. No one should force any fellow believer to act against his or her conscience.

In Romans 15:1–13 Paul concludes his exhortations on unity between the strong and the weak (*tōn adynatōn*). He identifies himself with the strong and speaks from experience by appealing to the strong Christians to bear (*bastazein*) with the failings of the weak and not to please themselves (Rom 15:1). They must not merely tolerate the weak, but they must also patiently and tenderly identify with them as much as possible, sacrificially accommodating the limitations of the weak members of the church (Rom 15:2). This exhortation is particularly applicable in Africa. By following it, the strong members of the church-family in Africa will be following the example of Jesus, who gave up his rights and put the interests of others before his own when he suffered and died for us (Rom 15:3). Paul draws from Psalm 69:9 to support his exhortation, showing that Christ's journey to the cross on behalf of others was an essential part of his mission.

In addition, Paul wants the church-family in Africa not only to practice ecumenism and Christian dialogue with other cultures, but to realize that Scripture, which focuses on Christ and the example the Messiah has set, is meant to build the virtues of endurance and encouragement in our lives (Rom 15:4). Maintaining these virtues, Paul prayerfully stresses, is necessary for the unity of members of the Church, who must bear with one another with love, acceptance, and tolerance (Rom 15:5–13)

SUMMARY

Although Paul's discussion of the weak and the strong deals with a practical issue, it raises important theological questions that are beneficial to the Church in Africa. Matera also expresses these questions. One such question is: What is the nature of the freedom that believers enjoy in Christ? This question arises because of Paul's teaching on justification by faith. If believers in the church-family in Africa are no longer under the law because they belong to Christ, then are they not free in regard to matters of the law? Again, since members of the church-family in Africa belong to the new humanity that their risen Lord has initiated, are they not free from all things that pertain to the aforementioned challenges plaguing Africa? In other words, can the freedom and new life that Christians in Africa enjoy in the Spirit be circumscribed in any way? While one can imagine that Paul would answer in favor of the freedom that Christians enjoy in Christ, his discussion in Romans 14:1–15:13 shows that there are moments when it is necessary to restrain one's personal freedom for the good of the body of believers.[17]

The freedom that members of the Church in Africa enjoy include the freedom to tolerate one another. They have the freedom to live in a community of Gentiles and Jews where each graciously acknowledges the differences of the other so that the entire community can worship God in the voice of the messianic Lord. Wright calls this freedom "shared worship."[18] It is a freedom that recognizes that, at times, it may be necessary to restrain oneself for the good of others since all are not at the same level of maturity in Christian life.[19]

In addition, Paul's vision for the church-family in Africa is characterized by love and encourages Christian ecumenism, intercultural dialogue, and religious dialogue. The church-family in Africa must transcend their tribal and sectional cultural differences and build a united and harmonious church-family rooted in the values of the gospel. It is this same vision of tolerance and unity that Pope Francis shares in his ministry.[20] With Paul, Pope Francis invites the church everywhere, and in Africa in particular, to go forth to eliminate division, promote unity, and be in contact with all peoples, both "the weak" and "the strong," and not only with a chosen or selected few.

17. Matera, *Romans*, 325.
18. Wright, "Letter to the Romans," 647.
19. Matera, *Romans*, 326.
20. Pope Francis, *Evangelii Gaudium*, nos. 38–47; Udoekpo, *Israel's Prophets*, 81–83.

A Modest Conclusion

THIS WORK SETS OUT not necessarily to ask all the questions nor to give all the solutions, but to study and explore some of the challenges facing today's desired unity, peace, and stability in Nigeria and beyond from a inclusive, contextual, biblical, and sociocultural perspective. The challenges identified in this text include social-religious, economic, and political challenges.

Regarding the social factor, we discussed family values and their contribution toward justice, peace, and unity in any nation. We argued that the family is the primordial community. It is the first and fundamental school of social existence or the primary vital cell of society. It is the backbone as well as the bedrock of the society. The family feeds the society with its fundamental constituents, human beings. The family and the larger society are so lined up that any progress or defect in one automatically reflects or metathesizes into the other. If the family gets forlorn and broken, then the peaceful continuity of the society is on fire for serious damage. However, many families today are disunited for reasons of infidelity to fellow partners, childlessness, the search for material benefits, lack of patience, intolerance, and a total lack of self-control. Therefore, a false family structure reflects the present-day society.

Regarding the religious factor, there is great disharmony and mismanagement among the different religions in Nigeria, including African Traditional Religions, Islam, and Christianity. The management of these complex religious groups, with their varying beliefs and values, is reflected in Nigerian political life. For instance, sometimes it appears that a person's position, power, authority, and wealth are related to their religious platform, passion, and sentiments. This is apparent in the religious riots we see in schools and institutions.

There is disunity among the Christian family. We see a proliferation of churches and groups on our streets and market squares. Many people want to be healed. They want to have vision, security, wealth, influence, prestige, power, honor, absolute freedom, and cultural identity.

Politically, all nations must strive to promote democratic principles and rule of law. In Nigeria and many other countries in the world, the road to unity with true political principles is still long. Some politicians who presumed politics to be a dirty game have done more harm than good in the search for unity. This work argues that politics is not a dirty game. It is not the art of the impossible. It is not violence. It is not the survival of the fittest. Rather, politics is a prudent search for the common good. Politics is not just good and noble of praise, but natural for the human person and society. Authentic politics, when conscientiously practiced, bring stability, love, and peace, and include the weak and the strong, black and white, male and female everywhere.

Peace is usually understood as that time when war or other such hostilities have come to an end. But a fuller understanding would include any time when two or more people are in a state of harmony and mutual agreement. Therefore, peace is not simply the absence of war. It is the biblical *shalom*, the care, compassion, and looking after one another. It is the kind of situation envisioned by the prophets, who depicted spears and swords giving way to implements of peace (Isa 2:1–4), who depicted people of different tribes, religions, and languages dwelling together in trust (Isa 11:4–11), and who spoke of righteousness and justice prevailing. When unselfish and informed love undergirds our political processes and economic systems, we have unity, peace, and justice. Unity also exists when justice, juridical activity, and rule of law are allowed to flow like an ever-flowing stream into all the nooks and corners of the earth (Amos 5:24).

In this search for unity, justice, rule of law, and peace, our media must not stand idle. The media must serve as good disseminators of information, news, and opinions. Our journalists must rise above abuse and promote a fruitful search for unity and stability. The media must remain the custodian of truth, development, unity, and peace.

To achieve unity and peace, we must eliminate such enemies as blind self-interest and corruption, as discussed in chapter five, including unbridled greed and tribal ambition. Corruption leads to economic exploitation, with the result that two out of three people go to bed hungry every night. It creates a chasm between the "haves" and the "have nots." Political oppression by corrupt officials is an enemy our desired unity because, through it, people are denied their basic human rights and justice, and consequently they fail to realize their full potential.

The morality tale in Judges 17:1–6, as discussed at length in chapter five, must serve as a lesson to us. Social, tribal, and ethnic discrimination as well as lies, like those Micah and his mother told, are enemies of people because they disturb domestic tranquility, contravene justice, and stand opposed to every communal, covenantal, and humanizing developmental process.

The teachings of Isaiah of Babylon (Isa 40:4–5) and the Evangelist Luke (Luke 3:4–6) in chapter six, and of Paul (Rom 14–15) in chapter seven, must be our guide as well. They must guide and challenge us to overcome obstacles to our authentic and intentional desire for unity in Nigeria and beyond. They must guide and challenge us as stress as well in the epilogue in working to bridge the existing socioeconomic and political gaps between the rich and poor, of different cultures, religions, and values. They must guide and challenge us to put limits to tribalism, ethnicity, racism, discrimination, and all forms of divisive and homophobic tendencies in our society. They must challenge us to give compassion a chance and recognize the need to always be our brothers' and sisters' keepers.

Epilogue

THE BOOK, *THE LIMITS of a Divided Nation with Perspectives from the Bible,* indicates the time to mark out the limits beyond which human acts must not supersede and to the heights human acts must aim at. While the title of the work pinpoints the negative consequences of a divided nation, it contents elucidate the factors responsible for the limitedness and points directly to their sources. It is therefore illusive to read the title of the work and presume to understand it as the usual analysis of the state of things in the society. The work goes far beyond a simple analysis of fact and a show of descriptive expertise. It proposes principles that guide human acts, indicates solutions and provides some necessary cautions through which the aspired values may be achieved and maintained. These facts make the work extraordinarily interesting since it concerns the human family, ethics, culture, politics and the society.

The family being the bedrock of values has all it takes to construct unity, peace and harmony in the society. It is, however, important to understand that the fabrics of good family are the prerequisites for the construction of a good society. The work clearly shows that when this foundation is destroyed, nothing built on its ruins can stand the taste of time. Society being built on the ruins of broken homes would only become a ruined nation. At the backside of this and a careful attention on the root cause of such phenomenon, there lies yet a pseudo-principle of absoluteness of freedom - a freedom without responsibility. A little annotation makes it clear: it is not irresponsibility that manifests itself, it is a total lack of and a steady maintenance of absence of responsibility. Irresponsibility is a momentary absence of responsibility, which presupposes consciousness of such status with a possibility of rehabilitation. But whenever freedom becomes an absolute guiding principle and detached from human nature, even human beings become autonomous in being and in acting. It is true that freedom is necessary in every human act, yet it must be *human freedom*. Detaching freedom from responsibility seems dangerous to any human family and nation. Obviously, this sets limits to the family in particular and to the nation in general.

In the post-modern Nigerian society, ethnicity is often confused with ethnocentrism. This confusion dates back to the era of the so-called Biafran war of 1967-1970 in which the northern part of the nation felt more Nigerian than the southern counterparts. The confusion brought out one of the most heinous civil war among the people of the same nation. Today the impact of such war is still felt all over the nation. Ethnicity is a natural endowment, an identity based on origin of which no one is responsible and of which no one has a freedom of choice over it. It is a sign of identification through which we can go back deep into our origin and personal history. Once it has adequately indicated one's origin, maybe through a tribal mark on the face, language, gesticulations, colour of the skin or any external documentation, its utility becomes exhausted. But when ethnicity is seen as an orbit on which all other cultures or ethnic groups rotate, a qualitative jump is being made into ethnocentrism. Ethnocentrism is that act of considering and putting more emphasis on one's culture as superior with respect to others. This, obviously, leads to particularism and anthropocentrism with all the ramifications and negative consequences. All along in the history of the world, ethnocentrism has spread its tentacles with different nomenclatures from slavery in the past centuries to the KKK of North America and down to the Apartheid of South Africa of the last century.

On another note, *The Limits of a Divide Nation with Perspectives from the Bible* intelligently brings to the fore yet an important fact that must be noted in trying to proffer solutions to conflicts and disunity among Nigerian States and regions. There is a common error of confusing religion with culture. This problem had existed during the monarchy period of the Old Testament and was successively corrected after deep wounds were made on the fabrics of history. The first error lies on the failure to understand that religion is not the *product* or an *epiphenomenon* of culture. Religion is an institution of its own, even though may co-exist with and can transform culture. Confusion between culture and religion breeds fundamentalism, religious fanatism and even terrorism as is being revealed in the present century. Religion and culture interrelate and co-exist, but they are not interchangeable in meaning, existence and contents.

The societies are organized with different policies through politics. Politics in its original meaning gets its strength from ethics and its specific aspiration to the common good. The source of strength and its aspiration are the major components of politics without which policies create division and conflicts. This fact, (disassociating politics from ethics and common good) has always been the problem of many political systems in Nigeria in particular and in the world in general.

Fortunately, in the midst of these limits, we find models from the Bible. Many socio-cultural and ethical narratives of the Old Testament bring forth new insights and formidable models of peaceful co-existence and unity among people. While the Old Testament provides the historical narratives of a divided nation, the New Testament provides ethical model for the construction of unity and peaceful national co-existence. *The Limits of a Divided Nation with Perspectives from the Bible,* written by a seasoned biblical scholar, Rev. Fr. Dr. Michael Udoekpo, serves as a ring of conjunction between the biblical truths and Nigerian socio-cultural facts and projects true model for solid national unity and peaceful co-existence.

Rev. Fr. Dr. Anselm Camillus Etokakpan
Department of Religious and Cultural Studies
University of Uyo

Bibliography

Achebe, Chinua. *The Trouble with Nigeria*. London: Heinemann, 1984.

Agbiji, Obaji M., and Ignatius Swart. "Religion and Social Transformation in Africa: A Critical and Appreciative Perspective." In *Scriptura* 114:1–20. Stellenbosch, 2015.

Aghaulor, Hyginus. *Communication Media in Evangelization: The Case of Nigerian Catholic Church*. Enugu, Nigeria: Bigard Memorial Seminary, 1993.

Alvarado Y, Ruth. "Facing Corruption Today in light of First Testament (Amos 8:1–7)." *Journal of Latin American Theology* 12 n. 2 (2017) 29–44.

Amit, Yairah. "Hidden Polemic in the Conquest of Dan: Judges 17–18." *VT* 40 (1990) 4–20.

Aranoff, Gerald. "The Connection between the Idol of Micah and the Concubine at Gibeah: A Rabbinic View." *Jewish Biblical Quarterly* 14 n. 2 (2013) 78–80.

Arroyo, Victor. "Corruption, Public Policies, and Ethical Challenges from Perspective of Christian Commitment." *Journal of Latin American Theology* 12 n. 2 (2017) 83–102.

Auld, A. Graeme. *Joshua, Judges, and Ruth*. The Daily Study Bible Series. Philadelphia: The Westminster Press, 1984.

Barron, Robert E. *Letter to a Suffering Church: A Bishop Speaks on the Sexual Abuse Crisis*. Illinois: Word on Fire Catholic Ministries, 2019.

Baumann, E. "תובש בוש , eine exegetische Untersunchung." *ZAW* 47 (1929) 17–44.

Becker, Uwe. *Richterzeit und Königtim: Redaktionsgeschichtliche Studien zum Richterbuch*. BZAW 192. Berlin: Walter de Gruyter, 1990.

Blundo, Giorgio, and Jean-Pierre Olivier de Sarden. "La corruption comme mode de gouvernance locale: Trois décennies de décentralization au Sénégal." *Afrique Contemporaine* 199 n. 3e (2001) 106–118.

Boling, Robert G. *Judges*, AB 6A. Garden City: Doubleday, 1975.

Borger, Riekele. "ובש בוש/תי." *ZAW* 66 (1954) 315–16.

Bracke, John M. "*šûb šebût*: A Reappraisal." *ZAW* 97 (1985) 233–244.

Braunik, Vincent. *Understanding the Historical Books of the Old Testament*. New York: Paulist Press, 2011.

Brettler, Marc Z. "Micah (Person)." In *Anchor Bible Dictionary*, edited by David Noel Freedman, 4:806–07. New York: Doubleday, 1992.

Briggs, Daminabo Sonny. *How to Fight Corruption in Nigeria*. Nigeria: Osia International Publishers, 2011.

Brown II, A. Philip, and Bryan W. Smith, eds. *A Reader's Hebrew Bible:* סיבותכו סיאיבנ. Grand Rapids: Zondervan, 2008.

Budde, Karl. "Ephod und Lade." *ZAW* 39 (1921) 1–42.

Bullón, H. Fernando. "Notes on Corruption in Latin America: Alternatives from Protestantism?" *Journal of Latin American Theology* 12.2 (2017) 11–28.

Burney, C.F. *The Book of Judges, with Introduction and Notes; and Notes on the Hebrew Text of the Books of Kings, with an Introduction and Appendix.* New York: Ktvan, 1970.

Benn, S. "Justice." In *Encyclopedia of Philosophy*, edited by Paul Edward, vols. 3&4. New York: Macmillan & Free Press, 1967.

Balch, David. "Luke." In *Eerdmans Commentary on the Bible*, edited by James Dunn. Grand Rapids: Eerdmans, 2003.

Baker, W. "Wilderness, Desert." In *Dictionary of the Old Testament: Pentateuch*, edited by T .D. Alexander and D. W. Baker. Downers Grove: IVP, 2003.

Bender, Harold S. *These Are My People: The Nature of the Church and Its Disciple According to the New Testament.* Scottdale: Herald Press, 1962.

Benedict XVI. *Africae Munus Post-Synodal Apostolic Exhortation on the Church in Africa in Service to Reconciliation, Justice and Peace, "You are the salt of the earth . . . You are the Light of the World (Matt 5:13–14)."* Vatican City: Libreria Editrice Vaticana, 2011.

Blenkinsopp, Joseph. *Isaiah 1–39.* AB 19A. New York: Doubleday, 2006.

Catholic Secretariat of Nigeria. *Church in Nigeria: Family of God on Mission. Lineamenta for the First National Pastoral Congress.* Nigeria: Catholic Secretariat of Nigeria, 1999.

Boff, Leonardo. *Church, Charism and Power, Liberation Theology and the Institutional Church.* London: SCM Press, 1985.

Branick, Vincent. *Understanding the Prophets and Their Books.* New York: Paulist Press, 2012.

Brawley, Robert L. *Text in Pours Forth Speech: Voices of Scripture in Luke-Acts.* Bloomington: Indiana University Press, 1995.

Bryan, Brendan. *Romans.* Sacred Pagina 6. Collegeville: Liturgical Press, 1996.

Bulletin of Ecumenical Theology 2. no.1. Enugu, Nigeria: Snaap Press Nig., Ltd., 1989.

Burnett, Clint. "Eschatological Prophets of Restoration: Luke's Theological Portrait of John the Baptist in Luke 3:1–6." *Neotestamentica* 41 (2013) 1–24.

Catechism of Vatican II. St. Paul's Publication, Dublin: Aiklone and Scepter Books, 1967.

Cazelles, H. "The Unity of the Bible and the People of God." *Scripture* 18 (1966) 1–10.

Chikwe, A. *Lenten Pastoral: Building the Church as the Family of God.* Nigeria: Snaap Press, 1995.

Chimtom, Ngala Killian. "On Easter, Nigerian Bishop Rebukes Religious Leaders over Corruption." *Crux.* https://cruxnow.com/global-church/2018/04/03/on-easter-nigerian-bishop-rebukes-religious-leaders-over-corruption/.

———. "Prayers won't eradicate Boko Haram, Education will, Says Nigerian Bishop." *Crux.* https://cruxnow.com/global-church/2017/10/21/prayers-wont-eradicate-boko-haram-education-will-says-nigerian-bishop/.

Chukwumu, F. "The Evils of Broken Families." *The Fountain. No 12; St. Joseph Major Seminar.* (1991) 17–27.

Chrysostom, J. *St. John Chrysostom: On Wealth and Poverty.* Translated by Catherine P. Roth. Crestwood: Vladmir's Press, 1984.

Cranfield, C. E. B. *A Critical and Exegetical Commentary on the Epistle to the Romans.* ICC. Edinburg: T&T Clark, 1975/79.

Crick, B. *In Defense of Politics.* Britain: Cox and Wyman, Ltd., 1962.

Culpepper, R. Alan. "The Gospel of Luke: Introduction, Commentary, and Reflections." In *New Interpreter's Bible*, edited by Lender E. Keck, 8:3–419. Nashville: Abingdon Press, 2015.

Das, Andrew A. *Solving the Romans Debate.* Minneapolis: Fortress, 2007.

David, J. "Marriage II Family." In *Sacramentum Mundi* 3 (1969) 223-4

De Lubac, Henri. *The Church: Paradox and Mystery.* Translated by James R. Dunne. Staten Island: Ecclesia Press, 1969.

Dempsey, Carol J. *Justice: A Biblical Perspective.* Missouri: Chalice Press, 2008.

Dempsey, Carol J., and Elayne J. Shapiro. *Reading the Bible, Transforming Conflict.* New York: Orbis, 2011.

Dietrich, W. L. שוב תובש, *Die Endzeitliche Wiederherstellung bei den Propheten.* BZAW 40 (1925) 33-37.

Deutsch, R. "The Biblical Concept of the 'People of God.' " *Southeast Asia Journal of Theology* 13 (1972) 4–12.

Donfried, Karl P. *The Romans Debate.* Revised edition. Peabody: Hendrickson, 1991.

Dulles, Cardinal Avery. *Models of the Church.* Expanded edition. New York: Doubleday, 2002.

Dorr, D. *Spirituality and Justice.* New York: Orbis, 1984.

———. *Integral Spirituality.* Dublin: Gill and Macmillan, Ltd., 1990.

———. *The Social Justice Agenda.* Dublin: Gill and Macmillan, Ltd., 1941.

———. *Option for the Poor.* Dublin: Gill and Macmillan, Ltd., 1992.

Edem, Michael. *Confused Values in Nigerian Context: Rituals Reveal Mythology.* Nigeria: Jeromelocho and Associates, Ltd., 1993.

Edisana Nwed Abasi Ibom. Apapa, Nigeria: The Bible Society of Nigeria, 1995.

Editorial, "The Role of the Church in the Fight against Corruption in Africa, *"Association for Free Resource and International Corporation (Afric),* 11.06.2019

Eddinger, Terry W. "An Analysis of Isaiah 40:1–11[17])." *Bulletin for Biblical Literature* 9 (1999) 119–135.

Etokudoh, Camillus. *Lenten Pastoral: Jesus' Priestly Prayer That They May Be One.* Nigeria: Ikot Ekpene Diocese, 1992.

Ekwelie, J. "Mass Media and National Development." In *Readings in African Humanities: African Cultural Development,* edited by Ogbu Kalu. Nigeria: Fourth Dimension Publ. Co., Ltd, 1978.

Elliger, K., and W. Rudolph, eds. הרות סיאיבנ סיבותכו, *Biblica Hebraica Stuttgartensia.* Stuttgart: Deutsche Bibelstiftung, 1967/77.

Faleye, Olukayode Abiodun. "Religious Corruption: A Dilemma of the Nigerian State." *Journal of Sustainable Development in Africa* 15 n. 1 (2013) 170–185.

Fewell, Donna Noland. *Reading Texts: Intertextuality and the Hebrew Bible.* Louisville: Westminster John Knox, 1992.

Fitzmyer, Joseph A. *The Gospel According to Luke.* AB 28–28. Garden City: Doubleday, 1981–1983.

———. *Romans.* AB 33. Garden City: Doubleday, 1993.

Francis O., Falako. "Religion as a Foundation that Destroys Corruption in Our National Development: A Christian Perspective." A paper presented at the 8th Annual Regional Conference of the Africa West Chapter of the J. Reuben Clark Law Society (JRCLS) on August, 18, 2017 at the Cultural Hall, Ikeja, Lagos, Nigeria.

Funk, Robert. "The Wilderness." *JBL* 78 (1959) 205–214.

Gray, John. *Joshua, Judges, Ruth.* NCBC. Grand Rapids: Eerdmans, 1986.

———. "Idolatry." In *IDB* 2:675–678. New York: Abingdon Press, 1992.

Grogan, Courtney. "Nigerian bishop condemns 'cries of shrill Islamization.' " *Crux.* https://cruxnow.com/global-church/2018/01/12/nigerian-bishop-condemns-cries-shrill-islamization/.

Haring, B. *Free and Faithful in Christ: Light of the World and Salt of the Earth.* Middle Green: St. Paul's Publishing, 1981.

Hays, Richard. *Echoes of Scripture in the Letter of Paul.* New Haven: Yale University Press, 1989.

———. *The Moral Vision of the New Testament.* San Francisco: HarperCollins, 1996.

HALOT. 2:546–547.

Heschel, A. J. *Prophets.* New York: Haper & Row, 1962.

Hess, Richard S. *Israelite Religions: An Archaeological and Biblical Survey.* Grand Rapids: Baker Academic, 2007.

Holladay, William L. *The Root Šûbh in the Old Testament: With Particular References to Its Usages in Covenantal Contexts.* Leiden: E. J. Brill, 1958.

House, Paul R. "Biblical Theology and the Wholeness of Scripture: Steps Toward a Program for the Future." In *Biblical Theology: Retrospect and Prospect,* edited by Scott J. Hafemann. Downers Grove: IVP, 2001.

Iloghalu, J. "Communication Media and Evangelization." *Wisdom Satellite* 3 no. 9 (1999).

Instrumentum Laboris of SECAM Golden Jubilee Year July 2018–July 2019, 3–5.

Introduction to Journalism. Unpublished lectures, Institute of Journalism and Continuing Education. Enugu, Nigeria, 1995.

Itebiye, Bernard O. "Corruption in Nigerian Society & The Insouciancing of the Church in the Light of Micah 3:9–12." *The European Scientific Journal* 12 n. 20 (2016) 317–328.

John, K. A. "Justice and Peace in the New Evangelization." *The Insight Magazine* 7. Nigeria: Claretian Missionaries, 1990.

John Paul II. *Laborem Excercens*: Encyclical on Human Work. Vatican City: Libreria Editrice Vaticana, 1981.

John Paul II. *Centesimus Annus: On The Hundreth Anniversary of Rerum Novarum* (Encyclical Letter May 1, 1991).

———. *The First African Synod, Ecclesia in Africa; Post-Synodal Apostolic Exhortation on the Church in Africa and its Evangelizing Towards the Year 2000; You Shall be my Witnesses" (Acts 1:8).* " Vatican City: Libreria Editrice Vaticana, 1995.

———.*The Family in the Modern World Encyclical Letter Familiaris Consortio.* Kenya: Pauline Publication, 1982, no.15.

Kasali, David M. "Romans" In *Africa Bible Commentary,* edited by Tokumboh Adeyome, 1349–76. Kenya: WordAlive Publishers, 2006.

Klein, Lillian R. *The Triumph of Irony in the Book of Judges.* JSOTSup 68. Sheffield: Almond Press, 1988.

Koet, Bart. "Isaiah in Luke-Acts." In *Isaiah in the New Testament,* edited by Steve Moyise and Maarten Menken. London: T &T Clark, 2005.

Komonchack, Joseph A. "The Catholic University in the Church." In *Catholic Universities in the Church and Society: Dialogue on Ex Corde Ecclesiae,* edited by John Langan. Washington DC: Georgetown University Press, 1993.

Labushchagne, C. J. *The Incomparability of Yahweh in the Old Testament.* Pretoria Oriental Series 5. Leiden: 1966.

Landry, Roger. "What to Do about Corruption in the Church?" *National Catholic Registrar.* www.neregistrar.com/site/print/58244.

Leuchter, Mark. "The Cult at Kiriath Yearim: Implications from the Biblical Record." *Vestus Testamentum* 58 (2008) 526–543.

Lohfink, Gerhard. *Jesus and Community: The Social Dimension of Christian Faith.* Philadelphia: Fortress Press, 1984.

Malchow, B. V. *Social Justice in the Hebrew Bible.* Collegeville: Liturgical Press, 1996.

Mallan, Peter. *The Reading and Transformation of Isaiah in Luke-Acts.* New York: T&T Clark, 2008.

Martin, Ralph P. *The Family and the Fellowship: New Testament Image of the Church.* Grand Rapids: Eerdmans, 1979.

Martens, Elmer A. "The People of God." In *Central Themes in Biblical Theology: Mapping Unity in Diversity,* edited by Scott J. Hafemann and Paul R. House, 224–253. Grand Rapids: Baker Academic, 2011.

Matera, Frank J. *Romans.* Grand Rapids: Baker, 2010.

Mbiti, John S. *Introduction to African Religion.* Bostwana: Heninemann, 1991.

Meek, James. *The Gentile Mission in Old Testament Citations of Acts.* New York: T &T Clark, 2008.

Minear, Paul S. *Images of the Church in the New Testament.* Louisville: Westminster John Knox, 2001.

Moo, Douglas J. *The Epistle to the Romans.* NICNT. Grand Rapids: Eerdmans, 1996.

Moore, Thomas S. "'To the End of the Earth': The Geographical and Ethnic Universalism of Acts 1:8 in Light of Isaianic Influence on Luke." *JETS* 40/3 (September 1997) 389–399.

Ndiokwere, N. *The African Church Today and Tomorrow.* Vol. 1. Prospect and Challenges. Nigeria: Effective Key Publ., Ltd., 1994.

Ngwoke, B. *Islam: The Q.I.C. and Nigerian Unity.* Enugu, Nigeria: Snaap Press, 1986.

———. "Christian Participation in Politics." In *Catholic Social Teaching En-Route in Africa.* Enugu, Nigeria: Snaap Press, Ltd., 1991.

Niditch, Susan. *Ancient Israelite Religion.* New York: Oxford University Press, 1997.

Noth, Martin. "The Background of Judges 17–18." In *Israel's Prophetic Heritage,* edited by B. W. Anderson and W. Harrelson. New York: Harper & Brothers, 1962.

Nwadiolar, Kanoyo Louis, and Charles Chukwuemeka Nweke. "The Relevance of the Church in Oppressive Situations: The Praxis Liberation Theology in Africa." In *Ogirisi: A New Journal of African Studies* 10 (2013) 79–96.

Nwachukwu, Fortunatus, ed. *One Faith: Many Tongues: Managing Diversity in the Church in Nigeria.* Abuja; Nigeria: Pauline Publications, 2017.

Nwoko, Mathew. "An Address to Media Men on Politics in the Fight for Justice and Right." In *The Brochure of the Launching of Basic World Political Theories.* Owerri: Claretian Institute of Philosophy, 1987.

Obiorah, F. *The Divine Deceit.* Nigeria: Optimal Publishers, Ltd., 1998.

Obunna, E. *The Root of Violence: A Moral Evaluation of the Nigerian-Biafran Civil War.* Rome: Gregorian Varsity Press, 1985.

Odili, H. *Sorrows of a Nation.* Enugu, Nigeria: Snaap Press, 1993.

O'Donovan, O. *The Desire of the Nations.* Cambridge: Cambridge University Press, 1996.

Okochi, A. "Religious Bias in Nigerian Politics." In *The Torch Magazine* 94. Enugu, Nigeria: Bigard Memorial Seminary, 1990

Okonjo-Iweala, Ngozi. *Fighting Corruption Is Dangerous: The Story Behind the Headlines.* Cambridge: MIT Press, 2018.

Okure, Teresa. "Church-Family of God: The Place of God's Reconciliation, Justice and Peace." In *Reconciliation, Justice and Peace: The Second African Synod*, edited by Orobator. New York: Orbis, 2011.

———. "Becoming the Church of the New Testament." In *The Church We Want: African Catholics Look to Vatican II*, edited by Orobator, 93–105. New York: Orbis, 2016.

Oji, Kanu Mazi A., and Valerie U. Oji. *Corruption in Nigeria: The Fight and Movement to Cure the Malady*. New York: University Press of America, 2010.

Onongha, Kelvin. "Corruption, Culture, and Conversation: The Role of the Church." *Journal of Applied Christian Leadership (JACJ)* 8/2 (2014) 67–82.

Onyumbe, Jacob. "Interrupting Our Journeys: Lamenting Political and Religious Corruption in the African Great Lakes Region." *Word & World* 37/3 (summer 2017) 263–270.

Olson, Dennis T. "The Book of Judges: Introduction, Commentary, and Reflections." In *New Interpreter's Bible*, edited by Leander E. Keck, 2:721–888. Nashville: Abingdon Press, 1998.

Orobator, Agbonkhiameghe E., ed. *Reconciliation, Justice and Peace: The Second Synod*. Maryknoll: Orbis, 2011.

Onyeocha, Marcel. *What Is Religious about Religious?* Claretian Publication Series. Nigeria: Claret ion Institute of Philosophy, 1992.

Padilla, C. René. "The Globalization of Greed." In *Journal of Latin American Theology* 9/2 (2014) 43–67.

Park, Eung Chung. *Either Jew or Gentile: Paul's Unfolding Theology of Inclusivity*. Louisville: Westminster John Knox, 2003.

Peschke, Henry. *Christian Ethics, Vol 2: A Presentation of Special Morality in the Light of Vatican II*. Dublin: C. Good Life Weale Akester, 1978.

Pope Francis. *The Joy of the Gospel, Evangelii Gaudium: Apostolic Exhortation*. Vatican City: Editrice Vaticana, 2015.

Preuschen, E. "Die Bedeutung von בוש תובש im Alten Testament." *ZAW* 15 (1895) 1–74.

Pillay, Jerry. "The Church as a Transformation and Change Agent." *HTS Theological Studies* 73/3 (2017).

Plato. *The Republic*. Translated by Benjamin Jowett. New York: Arimount, 1967.

Polzin, Robert. *Moses and the Deuteronomist: A Literary Study of the Deuteronomic History, Part One: Deuteronomy, Joshua, Judges*. New York: The Seabury Press, 1980.

Pope John XIII. Encyclical Letter: *Aaterna Dei Sapientia*, C.T.S., 1962.

Pope Paul VI. Apostolic Exhortation *Evangelii Nuntiandi; On Evangelization in the Modern world*. Vatican City: Libreria Editrice Vaticana, 1975.

Pope John Paul II. *The Family in the Modern World, Encyclical Letter Familiaris Consortia*. Kenya: Pauline Publication, 1982.

Poulin, C. *Salvific Invitation and Loving Response: The Fundamental Christian Dialogue*. Lagos, Nigeria: Ambassador Publication, Academy Press PLC, 1992.

Rahlfs, Alfred, ed. *Septuaginta*. Stuttgart: Deutsche Bibelgesellschaft, 1935/1979.

Rawls, J. A *Theology of Justice*. Cambridge: Harvard University Press, 1999.

Robbins, Vernon K. *Exploring the Texture of Texts: A Guide to Socio-Historical Interpretation*. Harrisburg: Trinity Press, 1996.

Schneider, Tammi J. *Judges*. Berit Olam Studies in Hebrew Narrative & Poetry. Collegeville: Liturgical Press, 1985.

Scott, Linday. "Political Corruption in the Gospels and the Book of Acts." *Journal of Latin American Theology* 12/2 (2017) 45–61.

Scott, William R. *A Simplified Guide to BHS (Biblia Hebraica Stuttgartensia): Critical Apparatus, Masora, Accents, Unusual & Other Markings.* Berkley: Bibal Press, 1987.

Smith, Daniel Jordan. *A Culture of Corruption: Everyday Deception and Popular Discontent in Nigeria.* Princeton: Princeton University Press, 2007.

Smart, Ninian. *Worldviews: Cross-cultural Explorations of Human Beliefs.* Third Edition. New Jersey: Prentice Hall, 2000.

———.*The World's Religions.* Second Edition. Cambridge: Cambridge University Press, 1998.

Soggin, J. Alberto. "שוב , Šûb, to return." In *TLOT* 3:1312–1317.

———. *Judges: A Commentary.* OLT. Philadelphia: Westminster, 1981.

So, Uwaifo. "Corruption and Nigerian Society: Biblical Perspective." *Journal of Sociology and Criminology, Social Crimonol* 6/2 (2018), 1–6.

Synod of Bishops, Second Special Assembly for Africa. *The Church in Africa in Service to Reconciliation, Justice and Peace.* "You are the salt of the earth. You are the light of the world" (Mt 5:13, 14). Vatican City: L.E.V., 2009.

Synod of Bishops, Special Assembly for Africa. *The Church in Africa and Her Evangelizing Mission Towards the Year 2000: "You shall be My Witnesses" (Acts 1"8).* In *Instrumentum Laboris* 25. Vatican City: L.E.V., 1993.

Täubler, Eugen. *Biblische Studien:Die Epoche der Richter.* Tübingen: J.C.B. Mohr, 1958.

Taylor, Walter F. Jr. *Paul Apostle to the Nations: An Introduction.* Minneapolis: Fortress Press, 2012.

Scobie, Charles H. H. *The Ways of Our God: An Approach to Biblical Theology.* Grand Rapids: Eerdmans, 2003.

Seufert, Matthew. "Reading Isaiah 40:1–11 in Light of Isaiah 36–37." *JETS* 58/2 (2015) 269–81.

Schofield, Alison. 'Wilderness." In *Eerdmans Dictionary of Early Judaism*, edited by John Collins and Daniel Harlow. Grand Rapids: Eerdmans, 2010.

Shaw, J. M. *The Pilgrim People of God: Recovering a Biblical Motif.* Minneapolis: Augsburg, 1990.

Ska. L-l. *Introduction to Reading the Pentateuch.* Translated by Sr. Pascale Dominique. Winona Lake: Eisenbrauns, 2006.

Spinoza, B. *The Theological-Political Treatise.* New York: Dover, 1951.

Stumph, C. *Philosophy, History and Problem.* New York: McGraw-Hill, 1971.

Sommer, Benjamin D. *A Prophet Reads Scripture: Allusions in Isaiah 40–66.* Stanford: Stanford University Press, 1998.

Talmon, Shemaryahu. "'The Sesert Motif' in the Bible and the Qumran Literature." In *Biblical Motifs; Origins and Transformation.* Cambridge: Harvard University Press, 1966.

The Catechism of the Catholic Church. Nigeria: St. Paul's Press, Ltd., 1994.

The JPS Hebrew-English Tnakh: The Traditional Hebrew Text and the New JPS Translation. Second Edition. Philadelphia: The Jewish Publication Society, 2000.

Uchegbue, Christian Onyenuaucheya. "The Place of the Church in the Socio-political and Economic Liberation of Nigeria." In *The Proceedings of 1st Annual International Interdisciplinary Conference (AJIC)*, held in Portugal (April 24–26, 2013) 141–154.

Udoekpo, Michael Ufok. *The Limits of a Divided Nation.* Enugu, Nigeria: Snap Press, 1999.

———. *Rethinking the Prophetic Critique of Worship in Amos 5 for Contemporary Nigeria and the USA.* Eugene: Pickwick, 2017.

————. *A Comparative Study of Annang & Judeo-Christian Conceptions of Unen (Justice).* Milwaukee: Sacred Heart Seminary and School of Theology, 2019.

————. *The Place of Mass Media Communication in Nation Building: Nigerian Perspective.* Nigeria: Bigard Memorial Seminary, 1993.

————. *Corruption in Nigerian Culture: The Liberating Mission of the Church.* Enugu, Nigeria: Snaap Press, 1994.

————. *Family Functions and Children's Education in Modern Society.* Ikot Ekpene, Nigeria: Patom's Graphics, 1997.

————. *Israel's Prophets and the Prophetic Effect of Pope of Francis: A Pastoral Companion.* Eugene: Wipf & Stock, 2018.

Van der Toorn, K., and Lewis. "סיפרת tərāphîm, דופא ʿephodh, דב badh" *ThWAT* 8:765–778.

Vatican II. *Dogmatic Constitution on the Church, Lumen Gentium,* 21 November, 1964.

Vatican II. *Pastoral Constitution on the Church in the Modern World, Gaudium et Spes,* 7 December, 1965.

Webb, Barry G. *The Book of Judges: An Integrated Reading.* JSOTSup 46. Sheffield: JSOT Press, 1987.

————. *The Message of Isaiah.* The Bible Speaks Today. Downers Grove: Inter-Varsity Press, 1996.

Weber, Robert, ed. *Biblia Sacra Iuxta Vulgatam Versionem.* Stuttgart: Deutsche Bibelgesellschaft, 1969/1994.

Wellhausen, Julius. *Die Composition des Hexateuchs und der Historischen Bücher des Alten Testaments.* 2nd edition. Berlin: Georg Reimer Verlag, 1889.

Wedderburn, A. M. J. *The Reasons for Romans. Studies in the New Testament and Its World.* Edinburgh: T & T Clark, 1991.

Wifall, Walter. *Israel's Prophets: Envoy of the King.* Chicago: Franciscan Herald, 1974.

Wilson, Michael K. "'As You Like It': The Idolatry of Micah and the Danites (Judges 17–18)." *The Reformed Theological Review* 54/2 (1995) 73–85.

Whybray, R. N. *The Second Isaiah.* New York: T & T Clark International, 2003.

Wosterstorff, N. *Justice, Right and Wrongs.* Oxford: Princeton University Press, 2008.

Wright, Archie. "Wilderness." *HIBD* 5 (2005) 848–854.

Wright, N. T. "The Letter to the Romans." In *New Interpreter's Bible,* edited by Leander E. Keck et al., 319–664. Nashville: Abingdon Press, 2015.

Wright, Christopher J. H. *Old Testament Ethics for the People of God.* Downers Grove: Inter Varsity Press, 2994.

Yee, Gale A. "Ideological Criticism: Judges 17–21 and the Dismembered Body." In *Judges & Method: New Approaches in Biblical Studies,* edited by G. A. Yee, 146–170. Minneapolis: Fortress Press, 1995.

Yoder, P. B. *Shalom: The Bible's Word for Salvation, Justice & Peace.* Indiana: Evangel Publishing House: Zürich: Lit Verlag GmbH & Co.Kg Wien, 1987.

Zevith, Z. "A Chapter in the History of Israelite Personal Names." *BASOR* 250 (1983) 12.

Index of Authors

Achebe, Chinua, 66, 86
Aghaulor, Hyginus, 51
Alvarado Y., Ruth, 58
Amit, Yairah, 60
Aranoff, Gerald, 66
Arroyo, Victor, 58
Auld, A. Graeme, 63

Baker, W., 77
Balch, David, 82–83
Barron, Robert E., 33
Baumann, E., 64
Becker, Uwe, 60, 63
Bender, Harold S., 75, 89
Benedict XVI, 71, 73
Benn, S., 12
Blenkinsopp, Joseph, 80
Blundo, Giorgio, 57
Boling, Robert G., 61, 63, 65
Borger, Riekele, 64
Bracke, John M., 64
Brettler, Marc Z., 61–62
Briggs, Daminabo Sonny, 55, 56
Boff, Leonardo, 40
Branick, Vincent, 58, 79
Brawley, Robert L., 72
Budde, Karl, 65
Burnett, Clint, 77–78, 80, 82–83
Burney, C. F., 63

Catholic Secretariat of Nigeria, 71, 81
Cazelles, H., 70
Chrysostom, J., 13

Chukwumu, F., 8
Cranfield, C. E. B., 87
Crick, B., 40
Culpepper, R. Alan, 76, 83

Das, Andrew A., 88
David, J., 43
De Lubac, Henri, 89
De Sarden, Jean-Pierre Olivier, 57
Dempsey, Carol J., 5, 21
Deutsch, R., 70
Dietrich, W. L., 64
Donfried, Karl P., 86
Dulles, Avery, 75, 82, 89

Edem, Michael, 14, 21
Edisana Nwed Abasi Ibom, 61
Ekwelie, J., 49–50
Etokudoh, Camillus, xix, 36

Faleye, Olukayode Abiodun, 55
Fewell, Donna Noland, 72
Fitzmyer, Joseph A., 80, 87
Funk, Robert, 77

Gray, John, 65

Haring, B., 42–43
Hays, Richard, 20, 72
Heschel, A. J., 77
Hess, Richard S., 25
Holladay, William L., 64
House, Paul R., 72

Itebiye, Bernard O., 55, 68

John, K. A., 12
Kasali, David M., 90
Klein, Lillian R., 65
Koet, Bart, 79
Komonchack, Joseph A., 71

Labushchagne, C. J., 61
Lohfink, Gerhard, 73–75

Malchow, B. V., 14–16
Mallan, Peter, 83
Martens, Elmer A., 70, 72
Matera, Frank J., 20, 86–88, 91–92
Mbiti, John S., 24–25
Meek, James, 83
Minear, Paul S., 75, 89
Moore, Thomas S., 63

Ndiokwere, N., 26
Ngwoke, B., 42
Niditch, Susan, 25
Noth, Martin, 60
Nwachukwu, Fortunatus, 71, 86
Nwoko, Mathew, 39–40, 52

Obunna, E., 41
Odili, H., 42
Oji, Kanu Mazi A., 55–56, 66–67
Oji, Valerie U., 55–56, 66–67
Okochi, A., 28–29
Okonjo-Iweala, Ngozi, 55–56
Okure, Teresa, 71, 75, 89
Olson, Dennis T., 59, 61–62, 65–66
Onongha, Kelvin, 68
Onyumbe, Jacob, 58, 69
Onyeocha, Marcel, 40
Orobator, Agbonkhiameghe E., 71

Park, Eung Chung, 4–5
Peschke, Henry, 7
Preuschen, E., 64
Plato, 11, 40

Polzin, Robert, 63
Pope Francis, 13–14, 71–73, 75, 84, 86, 92
Pope John Paul II, 2, 27, 42, 71, 73, 89
Pope Paul VI, 50, 73, 81, 89

Rawls, J., 12–13
Robbins, Vernon K., 72

Schneider, Tammi J., 58
Scott, William R., 60
Shapiro, Elayne J., 5
Smith, Daniel Jordan, 55–58
Smart, Ninian, 25
Soggin, J. Alberto, 64–65
So, Uwaifo, 55
Scobie, Charles H. H., 70, 74, 82
Schofield, Alison, 77
Shaw, J. M., 82
Spinoza, B., 12
Stumph, C., 11–12
Sommer, Benjamin D., 72

Taylor, Walter F. Jr., 86–88

Udoekpo, Michael Ufok, ix, xv, xx, 11–12, 14, 16, 29, 41, 45, 48, 55, 68, 77, 84, 92, 99

Van der Toorn, K., 65
Vatican II, 36, 73

Webb, Barry G., 60, 79
Wellhausen, Julius, 63
Wedderburn, A. M. J., 87
Wifall, Walter, 77
Wilson, Michael K., 66
Whybray, R. N., 79
Wright, N. T., 86, 92

Yee, Gale A., 62
Yoder, P. B., 18

Zevith, Z., 61

Index of Scriptures

GENESIS

1–3	4
4–5	4
6–11	4
9:1–17	74
11:30	10
12:1–3	74
12:2	82
13–14	4
15	74
17	74
28:5–22	4
31:19	65
31:34–35	65
37–50	4

EXODUS

3	78
19–24	74
20:1–17	55, 59
20:22—23:33	14
22:21	14
22:25	15
23:9	14

LEVITICUS

19:9–10	15
19:33–34	14
22	15
22:26	15
23:19–20	15
23:22	15

24:22	14

NUMBERS

6:24–26	xx
14:26–35	77

DEUTERONOMY

5:6–21	55, 59
9:7	77
10:19	14
16:18–20	15
17–26	14
24:1–15	15
24:10–11	15
25:13–15	15
24:17	15
24:19–22	15

JUDGES

1–16	59, 66
1:1—3:6	58n20
2:10–19	59
2:11	66
3:7—16:31	58n20
3:7	66
3:12	66
4:1	66
6:1	66
10:6	66
11	62n35
13	62n35
13:1	66

JUDGES *(continued)*

16:4	61
16:5	62
16:18	62
17–21	54, 58, 59, 65, 66
17–18	58n20, 59n21, 60n26
17	55, 56, 65
17:1–6	xvi, 1, 5, 42, 54–69, 95
17:1–5	61, 65
17:1–4	63
17:1–2	59, 68
17:1	61, 63
17:2–5	63
17:2–4	63, 64
17:2	59, 62, 64
17:3–5	59
17:3–4	54
17:3	62
17:4	61, 62, 63
17:5	63, 64
17:6	59, 61, 62, 66, 69
17:7–13	54, 59, 60, 62
17:12	65
17:13	59
18	62
18:1–31	60
18:1–6	60
18:1	59, 61, 62, 66
18:7–10	60
18:11–14	60
18:14	64, 65
18:15–20	60
18:17	64, 65
18:18	64, 65
18:21–27	59
18:23–26	60
18:24	54
18:27–31	59, 60
18:27	54, 59
18:30	62
18:31	64
19	62n35
19:1	59, 61, 62, 66
19:22–25	59
19:26–29	59
20:1–7	59
21:3	69
21:8–24	59
21:25	59, 61, 62, 66, 69

RUTH

2:1–11	19

1 SAMUEL

1:7	64
1:24	64
2:1–10	18
2:4–8	18
3:15	64
17:47	74
19:13	65
19:16	65
23:9	65

2 SAMUEL

7	74
9:12	61n28
12:1–4	19
23:5	74

1 KINGS

8:23–22	74
17:8–16	19
19:4–8	78
21	19
22	61n28

2 KINGS

22:12	61
23:24	65

1 CHRONICLES

5:5	61n28
9:15	61n28
23:30	61n28

2 CHRONICLES

19:5–7	19

EZRA

9:1–10	5

NEHEMIAH

5:1–13	19
11:17	61n28
10:12	61n28
13:23	5

JOB

31:16–20	19

PSALMS

10	17
10:4–6	17
10:8–10	17
10:12–15	17
22:22	74
33	18
33:5	18
69:9	91
89	18
89:3	74
89:5–14	18
89:28	74
94:5–6	18

PROVERBS

3:13–15	19
10:15	19
10:30–31	19
14:20	19
15:16–17	19
17:1	19
19:4	19
22:1	19
22:7	19
28:27	19
30:13–14	19
Ecclesiastes	
5:18–19	19
10:19	19
Isaiah	
1:17	16
2:1–4	94
11:4–11	94
29:21	16
39	79
40	82
40:1–11	79
40:1–2	79
40:2	79
40:3–5	78–84
40:3	76, 79, 80, 82
40:4–5	1, 5, 70–84, 95
40:5	82, 83
40:6–8	79
42:1–4	81
42:6	5
49:1–16	81
49:6	5
50:4–9	82
52:13—53:12	82
59:4	16, 17
61:1–2	20

JEREMIAH

2:12–13	77
22:13–17	17
33:21	74
Ezekiel	
21:21	65

AMOS

4:1	16
5	16
5:7	16
5:24	16, 94
8:4–8	77

MICAH

3:1–3	16
4:4	xvi
7	16
7:3	16

ZECHARIAH

10:2	65

MALACHI

3:1	76

SIRACH

13:21–22	19
30:14–16	19

MATTHEW

1:5	76
12:50	75
23:1–36	21
28:16–20	75
28:19–20	81

MARK

1:1	76
1:2	76, 79
1:3	76
1:4	76
1:5	76
10:28–30	75
16:15	27, 81

LUKE

1:16–17	76
1:17	80
1:46–53	21
1:51–53	83
1:54–55	74
1:76	80
1:80	76, 78
2:10–11	21
2:30–32	83
3:1–6	76
3:2	76, 78
3:3	76, 78
3:4–6	1, 5, 70–84, 95
3:4	76
3:5–6	70
3:5	82
3:8	78
3:10–14	78
3:21	76
4:17–21	20
4:24–30	83
4:42	78
5:16	78
7:27	76
13:29	83
18:1–8	21
23:26–43	21
24:47	83

JOHN

11:52	75
12:32	75
13:15	86
17	35
17:20–21	36
17:21	36

ACTS

1:2–7	83n64
1:8	83, 83n64
7:36–44	77n36
8	83n64
9:2	80
10–11	83n64
15	83n64
18:25	80
19:9	80
19:23	80
24:14	80
24:22	80

ROMANS

5:5	36
12:1—13:14	89
14–15	xvi, 1, 14, 84, 95
14	5
14:1—15:13	85–92
14:1–12	89
14:1–4	90
14:1	88
14:5–9	90
14:10–12	90
14:13–23	90
14:14–16	90
14:17–19	90
14:20–21	90
14:22–23	90
15	5
15:1–13	91
15:1–3	86
15:1	88, 91
15:2	91
15:3	91
15:4	91
15:5–13	91
15:7–13	90

16:1   75

1 CORINTHIANS

7:15   75
12:4–11   22
12:11   27

2 CORINTHIANS

5:17   81
5:19   75

GALATIANS

6:10   75
6:15   81

EPHESIANS

1:10   75

COLOSSIANS

1:20   75

1 TIMOTHY

2:4   27

JAMES

2:15   75

1 PETER

3:15–18   3

REVELATION

21:5   81

Index of Subjects

abuse, 2, 4, 39–43, 44–53
acknowledgements, xix–xx
adjustment programs, 67
adults, 9, 25, 72
Africa, xvii, 3, 7, 18, 24, 26–28, 46, 57,
    68, 71–73, 77, 79, 84–85, 87–90,
    92–93
  culture of, 10, 53
  church in, 5, 30–33, 76, 81–83, 90
African Traditional Religion, xii,
    26–28, 30, 93
analysis, xi, 68, 86, 97
anniversary, xix
anthropocentrism, 6, 98
apartheid, 3, 98
assembly, 74
authority, 8, 77, 93

beliefs, 10, 19, 24–38, 53, 93
Bible, ix, x, xii, xiv, xv, 1, 4, 18, 32
  story of the, 14, 19, 20, 82
  theology of the, 5
bless, xx
bribery, 6, 55–57

capitalism, 13
Catholic Church, 33–34, 70
challenges, 71, 82, 85, 92–93
children, xi–xii, 7, 9–10, 19, 50, 68, 72,
    74–75, 78
Christ, xix, 5, 20, 30, 35–38, 50, 70–75,
    77–78, 80–92
  way of, 81

Christian
  church, 35, 37
  communities, 33
  denominations, 37
  dialogue, 91
  ethics, 42–43
  people, xvi, 14, 34, 92
  religion, 26–30, 37–38, 87, 93
  society, 8
  unity, 36
church, 2, 31, 38, 74
  family, 71–73, 77, 79, 81–84, 88–89,
    92–93
  images of, 75
  nature of, 75
  universal nature of, 28
Civil War, 2–3, 98
classification, 12, 60n26
coexistence, v, xi–xiii, 2–3, 8, 25–26, 99
commandments, 10, 15, 55, 81
common good, xvi, 22, 42–43, 68, 77,
    85, 94, 99,
communication, 44–46, 49–51
community, xv–xvii, xix, 7, 27, 33,
    74–75, 82, 86–88, 91–93
commutative, 12–13
compassion, 2, 13, 77, 94–95
context, 4, 15, 27–28, 55, 58–59, 68,
    85–86, 90
converts, 28, 35, 87
corrective, 13, 72
corruption, ix, xvi, 2–3, 5–6, 41–45, 52,
    54–69

corruption *(continued)*
corrupt behavior, 54, 61
corrupt leadership, 62
forms of, 58
literature on, 55
couples, xii, 10
covenantal restoration, 79
culture, 4, 13, 33, 49–50, 53, 56, 58, 77,
84, 86, 88, 91, 95, 97–99
cycles, 66–67

democracy, ix–x, 41, 52–53, 78, 80
principles of, 94
Deutero Isaiah, 5, 72, 76, 79, 84
Deuteronomic tradition, 18, 58–59, 69
development, xii, xvii, 2, 8, 36, 45–50,
52
dialogue, xiii, xiv, 5–6, 26–28, 37, 72,
77, 81, 84–85, 89, 91–92
ecumenical, 36
didactic, 64
discipline, xi–xii, xiv, 66
disharmony, 1–3, 10–11, 22, 26, 38, 93
dishonoring parents, 64, 66
distinction, 13
distributive, 11–13
disunity, xii–xiii, xvi, 1, 3–10, 18, 22,
26–27, 29, 34, 38, 43, 54, 68, 80,
85, 87, 94, 98,
division, ix–x, xii–xiii, xix, 1–5, 9, 14,
26, 30, 33, 49, 71, 90, 92, 99
of homes, 9, 26
of the nation, xi–xii, xiv–xv, 85
causes of, xii, 22, 33–36

early media, 46–52
ecumenism, xiii, 6, 36, 91
education, xi, xiii, 6, 8, 49, 50, 53, 57
election, 4–5, 42, 57, 67, 82
epilogue, 97
epiphenomenon, 98
ethical implications, 89–91
ethnocentricism, xiii, xvi, 6
evangelization, 28, 49–50, 53, 72–73,
77–78, 80–81, 84, 89
exegetical theological, 68
exhortation, 15, 27, 88–91

factors, 4, 6, 9–10, 22, 30, 33, 97
faith, xiii, 6, 19, 25, 27, 31, 36–37,
49–50, 70, 72, 75, 90–91
family, xii–xix, 2, 6–23, 27, 34–35,
39–40, 50, 62, 68, 91, 93–94,
97–98
broken, 10
values , xiii, 2, 4, 6, 68, 71, 77, 93
fear of the Lord, 19, 54, 65, 67
financial system, 14
foreword, ix, xv
freedom, xvi, 9–10, 38, 43, 78, 90–92,
94, 97–98
fundamentalism, 2, 6, 14, 29, 98

Gentiles, 5, 22, 83, 85, 87, 92
God, xx, 55, 64–65
kingdom of, 49
justice of, 18, 20
people of, 53, 73, 74, 82, 89
saving activity of, 70, 89
government, ix–xii, 1, 21, 26, 28, 35,
40, 45–48, 52, 57, 67, 81, 88
grateful, xix

harmony, 2, 4–5, 7, 11, 21, 34, 53, 90,
94, 97
historical books, 14, 18
historical development, 45, 48
holocaust, xi, 2
house of gods, 63–64
human person, 2, 7–9, 27, 94
humanities, xvii

idolatry, 14, 54, 58–59, 64–69
Ikot Ekpene, xv, xix, 1–2, 28, 36–37
images, 59, 64, 72–73, 76, 84, 86, 88
inclusiveness, 21–22
independence, 34, 67
individualism, 13
infidelity, 3, 6, 9, 23, 93
information, 35, 45–52, 94
injustice, 3, 6, 11–12, 16–18, 41, 52
institutions, x–xi, 3, 22, 25, 39, 72, 90,
94
interim leader, 67
internal self-government, 67
intertextuality, 72n9, 76

intolerance, xvi, 29, 86, 93
Islam, xii, 26–27, 38, 93
  Assaults, 29, 93
  followers of, 14
Israel, 5, 14–18, 20, 61, 65, 69, 73–74,
    78, 83,
  religion of, 25
  king in, 59–69
  northern, 61
itinerant preacher, 78

Jerusalem, 16–17, 87
Jesus of Nazareth, 71
  priestly prayer of, 35–36, 38
Jewish Christians, 87–88
Jewish Sabbath, 90
Jews, 2–3, 5, 22, 85, 92
John the Baptist, 76–77, 84
Journalist, 48, 51
justice, 11–13, 15–17, 19–22, 40, 52,
    94–95

leaders , 21, 24, 28, 34, 38, 50, 59, 65,
    67–68
legislative texts, 14–16, 18
limits, ix, xi, xii, xiv, xv, xix, 1, 2, 32, 39,
    44, 68, 97

Magnificat, 18, 82
Management, 39, 46, 80, 93
mass media, xii–xiii, xvi, 1, 4, 43–53,
    68
members, xvi, 9, 12, 33–35, 42, 55, 62,
    72, 87–88, 90–92
Messiah, 37, 76, 91
metaphors, 72, 84, 88
Micah, 54, 59, 60–62, 59, 95
  confession of, 62
  household shrine of, 65, 68
  mother of, 54, 61–62
  name of, 61
misconceptions, 40
mission , 31
missionary, 27, 46, 72, 87
molten image, 54, 61–62
morality, xi–xii, 28, 41, 53, 68, 69,
  character, 62
  rights, 9

vision, 20
  tale of, 3, 5, 58–59, 62, 65, 68, 95
  teacher of, 55
mystery, 73, 89

nation building, 45
New Testament, 20–21, 70, 74–75, 99
newspaper, 46–48
Nigeria, ix–xiii, xvi–xvii, 1–3, 6–7,
    9–11, 13–14, 17, 21–23, 30, 38, 45,
    47–48, 50–51, 53, 56–59, 62, 66,
    69, 93, 99
  context of, 55
  culture of, 41
  society of, 98
  trouble in, 66
nongovernmental organization, 56
northerner, 14

obstacles, 42–43, 95
Old Testament, 20–21, 70, 74, 98–99
oppressed, 2, 16–17, 20, 29, 83
oppressors, 17, 29
organization, 34–35, 40

particularism, 4–5, 98
Paul, 14, 22, 85, 86–95
  community of, 14, 85, 87
  perspectives of, 84–85
peace, xi–xx, 2, 5, 8–9, 12, 18, 20–21,
    28–29, 35–36, 43, 51, 53, 71, 73,
    77, 81, 85–86, 89–90, 93–94, 97
peaceful, v, xii, xvii, 2–3, 8, 72, 93, 99
personal freedom, 92
perspective from Luke, 76
perspectives, 70
plan of salvation, 83
political structure, 6
politics, x, xii, 16, 28, 39–43
poor, 11, 13, 15–20, 22, 42, 52, 75, 77
poor and rich, 5, 12, 72, 83, 95
poor leadership, 59, 65–66
Pope Francis, 13, 71, 72, 75, 84, 86, 92,
prepare the way, 76, 78, 80
priests, xv, xix, 78
professional, 48
proliferation, 2, 85, 94

prophet, xvi, 16, 19, 27, 34, 72–73, 75–78, 84
prophetic books, 17, 78
prophetic mission, 77
publication, 51–50
publishers, 47

quest, 44–52

racism, xiii, 2–3, 14, 21, 95
reappraisal, 11–23, 55
reason, 46, 87
rectifying, 13, 21
refrain , 65–66
refrain-formula, 65
relativism , 6, 13, 54, 58, 65
religion, xii, 24, 29–30, 93, 95, 98–99
    Christian, 26–30, 37–38, 87, 93
    factors of, 22
    families of, 24, 31, 33
    groups of, 30, 35
    Israelite, 25
    new groups of, 34
    non-Christian, 27
    traditional, 93
repentance, 58, 64, 69, 78, 80
responsible factors, 9, 30, 33, 97–98
reproof, 54, 62
retribution, 12–13
revelation, 79, 83
right order, 12–13
righteousness, 16–21, 24, 89–90, 94
rituals, 25, 38

salvation history, 20, 74
Second Isaiah, 78, 81
service , x, xii, 8, 25, 43, 82, 89,
silver, 54, 60–64
social justice, 8, 12, 14, 18, 43, 67
socialization, 49–50, 52
society, xv, xvii, 6–7, 11–12, 23, 97
    Christian, 8
    contemporary, 8, 59
    disharmony, 11
    Nigerian, 98
    political, 39
    structures of, 23
socioeconomic, x, 88, 95,

sociopolitical, 2, 13, 34–35, 37, 58, 84, 86
solutions, 4, 30, 93, 97–98
southerner, 14
stealing, 54, 64–69
Suffering Servant, 81–82, 84
summary, 38, 43, 52, 68, 84, 91
symbols, 25, 72, 76, 84

techniques, 34–35, 48
temple, 16–17, 73, 89
Ten Commandments, 55, 59, 64
theft, 54, 62
theological commentaries, 73
theology, xiii, xv, 1, 4–5, 20, 72, 77, 84, 86
traditionalists, 30
traditions, xi, 18, 24–25
tribalism, 2, 14, 42, 52, 68, 71, 85, 95
typological forms, 57

unethical relativism, 54, 58
unfaithfulness, 58
United Nations, 7
unity, xi, xii, 7, 10, 19, 22, 30, 38, 44, 70, 73, 76, 93–95
    lack of, xiii, xvi, 4, 18, 43, 54
    national, 99
    promotion of, 49
universal God, 5
universalism, 4–5, 21–22
violence, x, xii–xiv, 2–3, 6, 14, 29, 34, 54, 58–59, 66–69, 71, 85, 94
virtues, 8, 91
vows, 65

war , xii–xiii, 2–3, 24, 31, 42, 45, 51, 54, 58, 71, 85, 94, 98,
weak and strong, 22, 85–86, 88, 90, 91
wilderness, 72–80, 84
wisdom literature, 14, 19–20
word of God, 76, 79, 83
working images, 88
worship, 9, 25, 27, 33, 54, 59, 61, 64–65, 74, 78, 85, 92
worship centers, 85
wrong, 12, 13, 24

youth, 8, 10, 22, 25